INVITATION TO JOY

In Praise of *Invitation to Joy*

In ***Invitation to Joy,*** *author John Murray offers winsome insights into navigating, with grace and empathy, the complexities of our world. From a rich and altruistic life, John has written with wisdom this heartfelt call to action, urging us to prioritize love, kindness, and respect in our interactions. He reminds us that our choices ripple through life, leaving a legacy of optimism and harmony. In a fractured world,* ***Invitation to Joy*** *shows us the path to a life of purpose, meaning, and hope.*

Dr. Ron Unruh, Author, and Artist

This book, ***Invitation to Joy,*** *is a thoughtful, honest, practical, and highly inspirational overview of the realities of life on earth and beyond. The writer's style is cordial and inviting, drawing the reader in to examine one's own life and future. Tough issues and hard questions are not avoided, providing credibility, authenticity, substance, encouragement, joy, and hope.*

Dr. Norman W. Ickert

In a convulsing world of pain and sorrow, inequality, injustice, violence and corruption, John Murray invites us to pursue joy-filled, purposeful living. John's insightful reflections help us see the positives in all-too-often negative circumstances. He reminds us that looking beyond ourselves, generously giving of our time and resources to help others, always ready to forgive and to be forgiven of inevitable failures is the route to a joyful, contented life.

While this call is open to all, John contends the ultimate joy-filled, purposeful life comes to those whose lives are fueled by a love for God found through a personal commitment to Jesus Christ as their Lord and Saviour. As with John's five previous books, and I've read them all, his writing is informative, challenging and encouraging. I encourage you to accept his Invitation to Joy.

David Daniels
Fellowship Baptist Pastor (Retired),
Freelance Writer and Reviewer

"With an honest recognition of the challenges and conflicts of life, John weaves together a collection of inspirational reflections that gently turn up the love, kindness, and hope dials. What emerges is an atmosphere and pathway to live a life of joy and peace, a life worth living."

Ray Vander Kooij
Senior Pastor,
Clinton Christian Reformed Church, ON

*John Murray's **Invitation to Joy** is a down-to-earth look at living a life of purpose and meaning. Anecdotal illustrations reflect upon a wide variety of people and how they have lived their lives, not just their main goal in life, but their daily choices. John challenges the reader to reflect on the spiritual side of life and what that means in terms of daily living. This book is well worth reading.*

David North, B.Ed., M.Ed. Retired Principal
Lions Gate Christian Academy

Through the telling of stories, both personal and learned, John Murray invites us to reflect on and recognize Joy! Not joy as a short-lived emotional response to a positive situation, but a deep-down contentment upon which a life can be both built and guided. For John, that profound joy is seated first and foremost in a personal relationship with Jesus Christ. We are living in challenging times, where anxiety seems to be so prolific. **"Invitation to Joy"**, *by its very title, invites us, reminds us, that the choice is ours as to how we respond to what life throws at us. The words contained within this book are encouraging, supporting, and uplifting. Oh, how we need these words today!*

Rob Ogilvie, Executive Minister
Canadian Baptists of Western Canada.

Through humble life experience and perspective spanning 85 years, John Murray has helped us all to understand that a life of joy is not so much the result of our own pursuit – sought for our own gain – as a product of choosing to love others. In the pages of **Invitation to Joy** *are written reflections, stories, quotations, and scriptures to guide us into understanding that the best self-help for achieving joy in our lives is living a life of self-giving. For it is as we engage with others using our God-given resources such as, personality, kindness, friendship, compassion, love, forgiveness, and more, we find ourselves fulfilled and enriched with purpose, meaning and joy!*

In these pages John has given us many of his own and others' life lessons as examples to gain appreciation for the truth of this book's focus – that true joy comes not from what is done for us or achieved by us, but how we treat others and what we do for them. It is this same self-giving sacrifice that Jesus demonstrated, and his apostles continued. No matter what stage of life you find yourself in, this book will be an encouragement for you to continue, or perhaps, to begin, an outward, others-focused life. For there is joy in this journey!

Gareth J Goossen
Pastor of Seniors Ministry
WMB Church, Waterloo, ON
Author of: *Worship Walk: Where Worship and Life Intersect*

Other books by John Murray

It's All About Love: Confessions of a Caregiver

Miracles: Coincidence or Divine Intervention

Real Faith: What's at the Heart of the Gospel?

Body Parts and the Invisible You

*Discover Your Hidden Self:
Finding Out who you Really Are!*

Information on these books is available at
www.jmurray.ca

INVITATION TO JOY

Your Pathway to a Purpose-Filled Life

John Murray

INVITATION TO LOVE
Your Pathway to a Purpose-Filled Life

Copyright © John Murray, 2023

All rights reserved. No part of this publication may be reproduced, stored in a retrieval system, or transmitted in any form or by any means, electronic, mechanical, photocopying, recording, or otherwise, without written permission of the author and publisher.

Unless otherwise stated, all Scripture quotations are taken from the Holy Bible, New International Version, NIV. Copyright 1973, 1978, 1984, 2011 by Biblica Inc. Used by permission of Zondervan. All rights reserved worldwide. The "NIV" and "New International Version" are trademarks registered in the United States Patent and Trademark Office by Biblica Inc.

Published by John Murray, White Rock, Canada

Cover design and photography by Roger E. Murray

ISBN
   Paperback   978-1-77354-529-5
      ebook   978-1-77354-528-8

Publication assistance and digital printing in Canada by

Contents

Introduction 1

We all come from somewhere 5

The tapestry of life 11

The building blocks of our society 17

What makes the world go round? 30

Love thy neighbour 38

Nothing is too small 49

Are we ever truly contented? 61

Can we afford not to give? 69

Attitude is everything 77

The comfort of forgiveness 86

No time to say goodbye 100

When things go wrong – and they do 107

That elusive purpose 123

Where do we go from here? 132

Afterword 145

Notes 147

About the author 152

Introduction

We live in a world where things are not right. It is a world that is rife with broken relationships caused by selfishness and pride. Our newscasts are filled with items of violence, inequality, injustice, and oppression. Sadly, many people are apathetic about the situation and are interested only in their own little world. There is no doubt that the world would be a better place if we had more love, kindness, respect, and consideration for each other.

It may be small, but I think we can all make a difference by showing that we care for each other by reaching out with love and kindness to those around us. I wish I had all the answers to the problems of our society, but I don't. However, I hope what I write in the following pages encourages someone to move forward, even minutely, in the direction of making a difference in our broken world.

Life is varied, and as with many others, our journey as a family has brought joy and pain, laughter, and tears.

It has provided times of rejoicing and times of sadness. We value the memory of the good times and appreciate that we were able to ride out the occasions we would like to forget. However, through it all, we have learned true values of life and the important issues that produce the backbone of a life worth living.

In this book, I would like to share some of those aspects that I consider important to a life of purpose and meaning. Not that I have attained being a perfect example of these principles over my eighty-five years, but by experience and by observation it is not difficult to see the results of your own actions and the actions of others. So, if there is one principle or suggestion in this book that you apply, and it improves your experience in life, then the book will have met its purpose.

Our lives today are the result of our choices made yesterday and we are subject to the consequences. Life itself forces us to make decisions as we go and we do, some good, some bad, with the corresponding results, some good, some not so good. We all make decisions based on the information we have at the time, but we must admit that not all work out for the best. Obviously, the better the choice, the better the outcome. However, the results are often beyond our control.

Invitation to Joy is about living a life that brings satisfaction and joy, but it is far from being a book about self. In fact, it's just the opposite. It's mostly about others and our interaction with them. I honestly believe that we can experience the joy of living as we put others first and show them due love, respect, and consideration, but more of that later.

This is not a self-help book. The first eleven chapters relate to our connection with other people; the last three have a more personal application. Hopefully, the book will encourage and challenge you to be the person you want to be and to be the kind of person you would like others to see. How often do we think about the impression we leave behind us? How nice it would be literally to leave a trail of positive vibes and a sense of appreciation from those with whom we cross paths.

I once knew a lady of whom it was said when visiting people, "She always left behind a special fragrance of gentleness, kindness and care." And it was not her perfume! It was her spirit. That was how she was. How wonderful it would be if people said something like that about us, that we left behind an air of genuine love, care, and understanding. Perhaps we should make that a goal.

Have you ever noticed the boomerang effect in life — we do something, and it reverberates back to us, either to reward us or to haunt us? I know in my attempt to be humorous I have said things that were inappropriate, and later regretted it. How I wished I had been more sensible, and especially more sensitive. Maybe you have done something similar and can identify with my mistake.

Our words and actions bring a consequence, either for others or for ourselves. Our reaction or response to life will produce a positive or negative outcome. Our relationships with one another are based upon many different aspects, some obvious and others not so much.

As you read the following pages, I hope you will see a reflection of yourself consciously putting into practice actions that will bring a rewarding and pleasing disposition in yourself, as well as provide closer and more meaningful friendships around you.

As the proverbial saying goes, the proof of the pudding is in the eating; thus, the joy of living is in the experience.

CHAPTER ONE

We All Come from Somewhere

With roots in the county of Essex in the United Kingdom, I have nothing but good to say about the English countryside. One would think that with a population of sixty-seven million people on such a small island, everyone would be standing shoulder to shoulder across the land, but of course that is not so. There are many thousands of untouched acres of land with forests, moors, streams, and lakes, and even a few mountains that rise to 4,000 feet in height. Across the country there are myriads of small farms and villages that add to the beauty of the land.

Our family came from a village that had turned into a small town by the time I left home. I think one would have classified our family as humble or lowly, and our upbringing reflected that status. For instance, for the first ten years of my life our family lived in a two-bedroom, semi-detached bungalow, on an unpaved road surrounded by fields. The house had only cold running water and no bathroom, just an outhouse – which was quite the wake-up call first thing in the morning, especially in the winter.

During those ten years two brothers arrived to join me, so by the time we moved there were five of us living in two bedrooms, a living room, and a small kitchen. It was a good thing that the local authorities built houses for those who desperately needed them after the Second World War. We were one of those families. So, in 1949 we moved into the luxury of a three-bedroom, semi-detached home with an indoor bathroom. Another brother came along after we had moved. My parents lived in that home until they passed away in 2008.

One of my joys of those early years was roaming the countryside looking for various birds, animals, and snakes. In fact, a playmate of mine at that time was bitten on the leg by a venomous viper snake and was taken to hospital. He did recover. Our house was not far from a river, so that also absorbed a good amount of our boyhood playtime. We lived next to a pig farm, and one of my delights was being allowed to help feed the pigs from about the age of six— not that I think I was a great help at that age.

In many villages throughout Great Britain, the local elementary school came under the jurisdiction of the Church of England. Until age eleven, I attended such a school. It had three classrooms. The headmaster, and later, the headmistress, conducted the morning opening assembly standing in the doorway between two of those rooms.

The church held some influence over the school. For instance, we students were expected to attend church services on the special religious days of celebration throughout the year, such as Ash Wednesday or Ascension Day. We would be marched up the hill, crocodile style, from school for the service (Anglican churches invariably stand on hills in England). The good thing was that we were always given the rest of the day off from school. Never understood that, but that was how it was. We children were also expected to learn the catechism, the Lord's Prayer, and other portions of scripture. I wonder how much of that memorization stayed with us children. It stayed with me for many years.

My parents were not highly educated. In fact, my father left school when he was fourteen years old and immediately went to work. Some years later, things had not changed much because I left school at age fifteen and immediately began work. However, later I decided to go to college before being conscripted into the British Army for two years.

Although my parents had minimal opportunity for education, that in no way reflected their lack of teaching us boys. Most things you learn and adopt from your parents come from non-verbal observation. In other words, without sitting us down and explaining how we should respect others, the example from their actions and attitude was enough to convey their thinking. The example of attitude and conversations spoke tacitly to their views and principles of living.

When it came to religion, our parents were devout Christians. Church played a prominent role in our lives as we grew up, with Sundays always being treated as a very special and sacred day. They may have relaxed by the time the last of us four boys had grown up, but I well remember not being allowed to play outside on a Sunday. Not that there was much time for that, anyway, going to church was an all-day event, even down to eating lunch and supper at the chapel. There were morning, afternoon, and evening services.

To get to the church, we either took the bus or walked the nearly two miles to the church. I remember those walks well, and especially the cold dark winter nights walking home during the black-out period of the war. No lights were allowed to be on in the streets or shining from homes, for fear the bombers would see populated areas. Looking back, and considering how it was then, it might be thought those Sunday activities were rather tiresome, but we knew nothing else, that was our way of life. However, I do remember enjoying the time spent with other young people of our own age at the church.

Was I influenced by my parents when it comes to the Christian faith? Undoubtedly, but only to a degree. During my early teenage years, I began to take in some of the teaching and came to recognize that, although my grandparents had been Christians, and my parents were Christians, it did not automatically make me a Christian. I discovered that there was no such thing as secondhand faith. I realized that the Christian faith was a personal matter, requiring a personal decision. So, I made that decision to become a Christian and was baptized into the Christian faith. However, that was just the beginning. I discovered there was much more to learn.

Ultimately, as the years passed, I discovered that the Christian faith governs your thinking and motivates your actions. Thus, my view on life is inevitably coloured by my belief system because that has formed the structure of my thinking, and consequently, it affects my writing. Just as one writer observes the world through his or her concept of atheism, so inevitably I view the world through the lens of the Christian faith.

My work years were spent in business, journalism, pastoral, and mission work. For my last twenty years of work, I worked with a mission in Eastern Europe, travelling from Russia in the north to Albania in the south. My speaking engagements took me to ten different countries, including Europe, the Caribbean, and North America. I only mention my work and travel to indicate that my observation of people and situations over those years has been varied and has influenced my views on life, which I think is reflected in my writing. You cannot be involved in physically giving food to the hungry without it creating gratefulness within you. You cannot experience seeing abject poverty without it causing deep appreciation for the privileged position we enjoy.

The purpose of this brief vignette of my background is simply to be open and honest as to my approach to life. It may appear simple, and it probably is, but I tend to compare the world as to how things are and how they could be or perhaps should be. I believe there are no areas in life to which the Christian faith cannot apply and make a positive difference.

You may or may not agree with me in what I write and that is fine, because that is your prerogative. We all have freedom of belief and freedom to disagree. You will find some of my observations are purely from a human point of view, while others are more spiritually derived. All are from my humble perspective of making the most of and finding the best in life, thus creating the experience of joyful living.

CHAPTER TWO

The Tapestry of Life

The world is a wonderful tapestry. Geographically, it offers us a superb variety of structures and colour, from majestic mountains to superb green valleys, from rushing and bubbling rivers to the calmness and serenity of a pristine lake. The multiple varieties of animals and birds add to that beauty and appreciation of creation. But the tapestry of life is also reflected in people.

We are all different and individually unique. Each of us is one of a kind. There has never been and never will be another you. Someone once said, "When God made you, he broke the mould." It's good to remember your uniqueness. God made you for a purpose. You have a special place here and are needed by those around you. We all come from vastly different family and cultural backgrounds. We have different personalities, different aspirations, and different beliefs. Yet despite that, we are all related as part of humanity. We all make up humankind.

In most major cities of the world now it is commonplace to find that your neighbour does not speak the same language as you. We have become a multicultural society and live in a cosmopolitan world. The differences in ethnicity and culture add beauty to humanity. Those differences add richness to our lives. While we appreciate the kaleidoscope of our differences, I ask the question, "Are we not all the same on the inside?"

Throughout life we all experience similar occurrences. We are born, and we die. We arrive the same way and we depart the same way. Therefore, is it not reasonable to assume that in between those events we all share the same struggles and have similar emotional experiences, both joy and turmoil? We laugh, we cry, we are glad, we are sad, and commonly encounter all other aspects of life.

When we see on the news the devastation from mud slides, typhoons, floods, and earthquakes, is not the despair of homelessness or loss of life identical wherever it occurs? The grief of losing loved ones to death is just as unbearable the world over. We can all readily identify with pain and suffering. It is universal.

Poverty and starvation are all too common now. Drug addiction is rampant. Mental illness is another scourge many people suffer. Thousands of people seek refugee status in the hope of improving their lives, as anything is better than what they have. People are disillusioned. They feel lost. They need love, understanding, kindness and support.

As part of humanity, we all experience serious disappointments, illness, accidents and other upsetting and disturbing situations. We all have dreams and hopes for the future. We all carry hurt and fears. In different ways, we are all vulnerable. We all must deal with age-related problems of our own or those of our parents. Experiencing such similarities, how then do we view one another?

There is little question that some of us approach others with pre-conceived notions and views, particularly in terms of ethnicity. We tend to compartmentalize people. We are often guilty of stereotyping people or carrying underlying prejudices. One bad apple in the bag does not mean that the whole bag of apples is bad. Sometimes it surprises us when a person turns out to be completely different to what we had assumed. We naturally make assumptions and often jump to conclusions by what we see, or what we think we see, or what we know or think we know. It is true that first impressions tend to stick, but we must admit that occasionally we are wrong in our assumptions and characterizations. All people deserve dignity and respect.

The value of a person is not measured by where they come from. Nor is it measured by their ability to achieve or even their ability to create. We are not valued by what we do, or what we can do, but by who we are—simple human beings with faults, failings, and foibles. As such, there is a certain equality among us all. Some may be better educated than others and hold higher positions in business or other organizations, but it makes no difference when it comes to being human. We all must get up in the morning, get dressed, brush our teeth, have breakfast, and so forth. The differences are all washed away as we stand naked from any trappings. We need to recognize the inherent value of every person; none is excluded.

It is we who have categorized and mentally set people apart. It is we who venerate people to pedestal positions. We put sports personalities and actors into prominent positions of adoration. People in powerful positions of leadership are given far more than simple respect. Some are even considered untouchable, as though they are superior to the common man or woman. It is hard for us to comprehend that the shoeless little boy in the jungles of Cambodia or South America is no different in the sight of God than the President of the United States. Equality is the name of the game in our humanness, regardless of position, power, or possessions.

Have you ever tried to identify with a specific group of people? I have. I have tried to get into the mind of a refugee, trying to imagine their situation and their inner sense of hopelessness and helplessness. I have heard of refugees forced to leave their home at gunpoint with ten minutes' notice. I have tried to imagine myself in that position and wondered what I would grab first to take with me. What do you do? Where do you go? You have no home, and very soon, no country. Where is your next meal coming from? How will you feed your children? You wander with others, not knowing where you will end up. Unwanted by most countries, you are forced to rely upon the goodness and kindness of those who will step up to help. Thousands of people suffer such a plight today, and I would not wish any of it on anyone.

Truthfully, we don't always understand the idiosyncrasies or ways of some people, but that should not preclude our acceptance of them. We can never truly understand someone unless we are able to get into their shoes, feel what they feel and fully know what issues they face. Because of our ethnic, cultural, and religious differences, it is impossible to think the same and agree on every issue. But people are people, and as such deserve our due consideration. To build relationships with those of a different nationality, different cultural upbringing, a difference in ethnicity or religious persuasion, takes empathy, open mindedness, and understanding.

So then how should we look at each other? I believe with an openness, with absolute respect, with an attitude of acceptance, and an uncritical spirit. We should not make assumptions without having all the facts. We need to hold a balanced perspective and a fair view of everyone we meet, recognizing that we are all human, we all make mistakes, and very often need forgiveness. We are all on the same level. As such, none is better than another. Realizing that should keep us humble.

CHAPTER THREE.

The Building Blocks of Our Society

Have you ever considered that relationships form the structure of the world as we know it? From our families, our friends, our work colleagues, our churches, the organizations across our country, even to nations around the world, relationships are the basis for all our communications. They exist either as friendships and provide cooperation, or enemies and create animosity. I sometimes think that our society is marked more by hostility than understanding and cooperation. That is the big picture, and in that picture, we see the desperate need for building and developing good relationships between people and countries. Sadly, the inter-racial and inter-ethnic relationships leave much to be desired today. However, our consideration here concerns personal relationships, mostly those within our families and among our friends.

The primary pillar for enjoyable living is solid, first-class relationships between one another. Without them, life can be miserable. I like what I read about Charlie Brown's young friend Linus, who told his sister he wanted to be a doctor. Her response was, "You could never be a doctor because you don't like humankind." To which Linus replied, "I do too love humankind. It's people I can't stand!" Loving humankind might be easy, but building and maintaining personal relationships is sometimes more difficult, but very essential. Dr. Albert Schweitzer once made a very telling statement. He said, "We are all so much together, but we are all dying of loneliness."[1] I am not sure about the "all," but I am certain there is much truth in what he says.

We were made for relationships with one another. They are essential to our well-being. We need that sense of belonging. We start out that way with the mother and child relationship. It grows and develops from there. Relationships form a strategic part of our daily living. We rely upon those in whom we trust. Loving and amiable relationships within the home are the basis of a happy home. Good relationships with work colleagues make for a pleasant working environment. Most of us probably have experienced work relationships that have not been so good. They leave us less than keen to interact with others in a potentially toxic atmosphere.

Good communication is the name of the game when it comes to forming and maintaining good relationships. Unfortunately, the failure of many relationships is often a simple misunderstanding, which is normally created by a lack of communication. How often have we heard, "That's not what I meant," or "I had no idea that is how you felt," or "Why didn't you say that?" An honest sharing of facts and feelings lays the groundwork for healthy, open communication and is the basis for good relationships.

Sometimes we do not reveal all the details of an issue because we are unsure of how our words will be received. We surmise that the other person will pick up the wrong meaning, question our motive, or take things the wrong way, possibly just opposite to our real intent. But by not saying anything, we find we are left with a greater exposure to potential misunderstanding. Then we wish we had spoken up openly and honestly in the first place. Not that we were being dishonest but thought we knew the reaction our comments would bring. Then we hear those words, "I wish you had said that in the first place; we would not have misunderstood as we did."

As we interact with others, we give them an image of ourselves. People quickly gain a picture of who we are, how we think, and our attitude to various aspects of life. It happens. We have no choice. We talk, act, gesticulate, and display body language that speaks volumes. What it says is important. What would you like it to say? "I am your friend. I care about you. Tell me truthfully how you are. Tell me honestly about your situation!" We certainly don't want it to say, "Listen to my tale of woe. My concerns are greater than yours," or similar sentiments. Our interaction needs to be open and honest and show genuine concern.

I have considered for many years that relationships are the most important aspect of our lives. It doesn't matter who we are, what position we hold, how high our rank is in society — without good relationships we have very little in life. Relationships are more important than money. What worth is money in the bank if you have no family or friends? It is never wrong to want to have a good job, do a good job, and work for a position of leadership, but I would suggest it never be at the cost of relationships with family or friends. Good relationships cannot be bought; they are the result of mutual appreciation, admiration, and respect, as well as the investment of meaningful time together.

Within the Family

Let's look at family relationships for a few moments. As we observe others, it's not uncommon for us to look from the outside and surmise that we are looking at the "perfect family." But does the perfect family really exist? As humans, most of us have our foibles and idiosyncrasies, some of which cause waves of uneasiness and even disturbance in the family setting. Teenage growth and development can create huge rifts within the family circle. Hurtful things are said and done only to later bring regret. Apologies suffice until next time—and there usually is a next time.

It's critical that every member of the family feels loved and supported, especially when there is pressure from outside the family, such as from the workplace, studying, examinations, job interviews, changing jobs, romantic involvements, and other aspects of everyday life. It takes extraordinary love and patience when views differ, and when certain family members seem not to be on the same page.

It is very hard to watch someone go down what we might consider to be the wrong road. That's the time we feel desperate to offer some wise advice. Yet we know it is imperative that even our family members must discover for themselves that there is a better way. I once heard it said that it is not until young people have children of their own that they suddenly realize their parents were not so "out to lunch" as they had thought. Looking back, they think their parents, surprisingly, showed some real wisdom. There are times when advice is all we can give, and even that is not always appreciated. But that is one side of the coin.

It sometimes happens the other way around also. I know of a situation where a young man tried to seek guidance and assistance from his father about certain things going on in his life, but the help was not forthcoming because of busyness. The father was on virtually every church board that existed and was out almost every night doing "church stuff," until one evening the son lost it and in an outburst at the dinner table, shouted, "Not another meeting. Are you ever going to be in? I need help!" Fortunately, the father recognized his responsibility to his son and family. He immediately took steps to right the situation and the young man got the help he needed. We can be too busy even doing good things.

Knowing our children is almost impossible. It is difficult to know at times what is going on in their mind. Even when we show a willingness to be open and listen—which is what they need—it is not always as successful as we might hope. But listen we must because listening indicates that we care. Some children experience a sense of isolation even within their own family. In the vortex of busyness, they feel that they are not being heard, hence our need for giving undivided attention and listening beyond their words.

Naturally, parents have a tremendous influence on their children, but what can be so easily overlooked is the silent transference of attitude. Without saying a word, a parent can pass on an attitude, either relating to the child, to the other parent, to someone outside the family, or even to life itself. Some conveyed attitudes can be extremely negative and limiting upon children. What we are speaks louder than what we say. It's critical that during the early development years the child does not pick up a negative view of themselves. Those are the impressionable years when children tacitly pick up parental or adult attitudes about themselves, whether verbally spoken or not. Psychologists suggest that our personalities are formed by the time we are six years old. Another reason for good parental influence in the early years.

Some while ago, I read that a child, especially under the age of three, can be emotionally damaged quite unwittingly by an angry parent overreacting to some small misdemeanor. The child reads the face and hears the anger in the voice and interprets it as "I am not loved." Apparently, it takes very few such outbursts to solidify a long-term negative sense within a very young child. Correction and discipline always call for thoughtful and wise application.

There are so many ups and downs and constant changes within families that it is virtually impossible to keep everything running smoothly. It takes effort and hard work to ensure that every member of the family receives the time due to them. Each spouse and each child have issues which call for due consideration at some point from other members of the family. Everyone needs to be assured that help is there for them at the appropriate time.

To be available is the prime order of the day. In busy families, time seems to be at a premium, but parents need to find the time if each member is to be respected and their needs are to be met. Sometimes less is more. The fewer activities, the more time spent together. Nobody wants to restrict their child from being involved in activities they love, but it can get out of hand and the parents simply become unpaid chauffeurs.

Quality time together as a family is critically important. It is the time when stories can be told, games can be played, and a genuine interest shown in each other's activities. It shows care for one another. It's a time for building trust, for showing understanding, and for being approachable, all of which are essential for good communication. It provides an opportunity to appreciate the different strengths and abilities of each family member. It creates a sense of belonging together as a family. Such family times where laughter is present display the love that binds the family together. One teenager, in a moment of honest disclosure, shared, "If we could not laugh together around this table, I couldn't stand this family." A little harsh maybe, but it highlights the need for remaining close together. There once was a popular phrase that said, "The family that prays together stays together." Someone changed it to "The family that plays together stays together." I think both are true because every family needs prayer and laughter.

How well do we know each other, even within the close family circle? I heard once that you are not close enough to your children unless you know the names of their friends. Family life is a never-ending "learning on the job" situation. Just as life itself does not always prove to be easy, so family life is not always easy in attempting to keep the boat on an even keel. It takes effort and often hard work; however, all the effort expended is an investment that will produce dividends lasting a lifetime.

Christian families are not impervious to the difficulties found in every family. In an atmosphere where the love of Christ would generally be seen and felt, the differences in personalities and attitudes can be the cause of abrasive relationships. It often takes a humble attitude and self-sacrifice to smooth out potential rifts. The purposeful demonstration and display of humility, compassion, and the love of Christ will do wonders for creating an environment of forgiveness. An air of peace will also pervade the home. As the scripture says, "Be completely humble and gentle; be patient, bearing with one another in love." (Ephesians 4:2 NIV) I know that applies to all people, but it has a particular application within the home.

With Friends

From what I understand, friendship, kindness, and acceptance are among the most longed-for aspects people crave. The value of true friendship can never be overestimated. Such friendship gives us support and helps to build us up. Toxic friendships do the opposite. They pull us down and can destroy us. Interaction with non-family members is important to help shape our thinking and gain concepts of the world and the views of others. We gain knowledge and experience as we associate with friends. But true friendship is more than that.

Sad is the person who does not have a bevy of friends. Most of us do, although there is often a fine line between friends and acquaintances. We may know many people, but how do you define who are friends and who are acquaintances? On someone's Facebook page, I noticed that they have almost 5,000 friends. I would doubt that. Can you really know that number of people? It's true that they may be acquainted with you and have chosen to be a follower, but to know that huge number of people personally would be difficult.

It takes effort to cultivate and maintain friendships. Keeping in touch with people takes determination. For most people, the Christmas card has been the number one annual link, although that has now diminished in recent years, with email taking its place. So, what is that relationship we call friendship?

How do we define a friend? I would say I know several hundred people, particularly through church connections, but trying to measure who would classify themselves as a friend of mine is difficult. I try to think of who

I could call on the telephone and they would answer "Oh, hello John, nice to hear from you," as opposed to, "Oh my, John Murray, what do I owe this call to, what have I done wrong?" or even worse, just, "Who did you say you are?" Obviously, the first group seemingly acknowledges our friendship, while the second group virtually indicates being an acquaintance. Acquaintances are numerous, but real friends are few. Obviously, the third group has no recognized established connection with me. But friendship is more than just knowing people.

In a previous book, *Body Parts and the Invisible You*, I wrote these words about friendship. "Friends are those with whom we have invested time and effort to be with regularly and enjoy their company. This builds understanding and trust. It has been said that a real friend is someone who knows all about you and loves you anyway. Real friendship does not change with fluctuating circumstances. A real friend will stand by you, will stand with you, and will uphold you in the tough times. It is seen in their kindness, their empathy, and their love. They will bail you out in times of hardship and will lift you up when you fall down. Such friends will give support at the best of times and at the worst of times. They will give and not look for compensation."

I answered the phone one day only to be surprised to hear the voice of a friend who I knew to be in hospital. His words were, "Will you come and see me, John.

I am not long for this life and would like to see you." I immediately went to the hospital. He simply wanted to say goodbye and to thank us for the friendship my wife and I had given him. Apparently, it had been very meaningful to him, much more than we had understood. I asked him how he felt. He said, "I feel like I am living in a bubble of peace." What a wonderful sense to have just a few days before leaving this life.

As we get older, our circle of friends shrinks. It's one of those inevitabilities over which we have no control. It's accentuated if you or your friends must move geographically for family or health reasons. Unfortunately, friends also die and leave a sad gap in our life. It pains us when we lose them. There are times in life when we need to make the effort to form new relationships and build new friendships. Coming out the other side of a traumatic event, like a divorce, the death of a loved one, or some other equally devastating event, it's common to experience a sense of loneliness. We may feel the need to fill that emptiness and building new friendships might be the thing to do.

Finding new friendships is not easy but it has proven to be a blessing for many who have gone out of their way to acquire them. Surprisingly, you may find it achieves much more than you expected. You might discover that someone out there may desperately need your friendship. By giving we receive. By reaching out, others reach back. Both benefit. The place to start is, naturally, finding people of common interest. Think about an evening class in a subject or craft you enjoy. Join a church study group. Volunteer at your local hospice. Volunteer at your local food bank. Offer to help at your local hospital. You will find others of like mind and having the same interests. The time, energy, and effort you put in to socializing and mixing with others will bring its own reward, along with new, caring, and understanding friends.

True friends are invaluable. They are like diamonds—priceless! You can trust them, rely on them, confide in them. You can lean upon them. You will find them by your side in a crisis. Friends like that are worth their weight in gold and are to be truly valued. Don't lose them. They are hard to replace. Someone has said, "You can buy friends, but not good ones!"

CHAPTER FOUR

What Makes the World Go Round?

A very old song declared, "Love makes the world go round." Maybe that is not so in practical terms, but we understand the sentiment. Can you imagine a world without love? It's hard to conceive and certainly would not make for a pleasant existence for any of us. Perhaps love is an invisible glue that creates a certain stability in society. Who knows?

Love can represent something exquisitely beautiful, but it can also be the instigator of jealous fits of rage resulting in a crime of passion. Love is such a small word but used millions of times a day around the world. It's probably the most used word ever. The subject is almost certainly the most popular. In a book of quotations, I found over 300 entries on love, which far exceeded any other subject. Hundreds of thousands of books are published annually, a high proportion of which would be romance novels along with non-fiction books and films also covering the subject of love. For centuries, it has been the subject of literature, plays, songs and operas. *Romeo and Juliet* readily comes to mind.

All love is not the same.

Love comes in many forms. We have a love for people, for animals, for hobbies, for sports, and a real love for food, and so on. But what distinguishes love from like? Although we use the word *love* readily, there are situations and subjects where we would probably replace *love* with *like*. When we like something, we find it enjoyable or preferable over something else, whereas love is a deep affection for something or someone, even to the point of passion.

C. S. Lewis wrote a book entitled, *The Four Loves*, in which he discusses what he sees as the four aspects of love. He names them as affection, friendship, eros, and charity. Obviously, love for our spouse, parents, and children is different from love for friends, just as romantic love is different again from love for others in general. Love has also been broken down into slightly different categories—romantic, family, friendship, and spiritual or supernatural. Different people in our lives call for a distinctive form and level of love.

Love is immensely important to all of us. From our earliest days, we all have had a deep desire to love and be loved. I believe that originates from the fact that we were created for love and to be loved. Sadly, we seem to have fallen somewhat short in that department. The violence in our world demonstrates an underlying hatred. It's a sad commentary on our society when murder and mass shootings become a common occurrence. That was not the plan. The plan was that we would experience love and harmony.

The need for acceptance and love appears to be deeply embedded in our psyche. In fact, when love and acceptance are lacking, it can create serious psychological problems. Such is its importance in our lives. Love brings happiness, contentment, and confidence. It creates security in the one who is loved. But none of this happens without the outward expression of love.

I used to wonder whether love is love if it is not expressed. If it is not expressed, then where is it? In the heart, in the mind? But does it really exist until it's known by the object of that love? I really believe the love is already there in the heart, although I like the words of a song by Oscar Hammerstein II.

> *A bell's not a bell 'til you ring it*
> *A song's not a song 'til you sing it*
> *Love in your heart wasn't put there to stay*
> *Love isn't love 'til you give it away.*

Strange, isn't it, to think that love is something you must give away to prove its existence. And that is what we are called to do, to give our love away. I think that love is love when it hits the road and becomes a reality in someone else's life.

Many years ago, Mother Teresa made this very pertinent statement that still has application today. She said, "The greatest disease in the West today is not TB or leprosy, it is being unwanted, unloved, and uncared for. We can cure physical disease with medicine, but the only cure for loneliness, despair, and hopelessness is love. There are many in the world who are dying for a piece of bread, but there are many more dying for a little love. The poverty in the West is a different kind of poverty; it is not only a poverty of loneliness but also of spirituality. There's a hunger for love as there is a hunger for God."[1]

The outward expression of love is powerful. It carries an extremely positive emotional effect upon the recipient. It comforts, brings strength, consolidates relationships, and establishes new ones. Yet how reluctant we are to utter those three little words, "I love you." If "I'm sorry" are the hardest words to say, then "I love you" should be the easiest, but that doesn't always seem to be the case. I believe we now live in a society where the phrase is used far more than it once was. It is now quite a common occurrence to hear "Love you" along with a goodbye.

However, there are those who still find the words stick in their throat because of other relational issues.

There is a wonderful story of love taken from a 1983 novel by Alan Paton entitled, *Ah, But Your Land Is Beautiful*. It features a girl with a terrible facial disfigurement and a blind man who fell in love and married. One day a surgeon examined the man's eyes and said, "I believe I can restore your sight." The man was overjoyed but his wife was gripped by fear. Sensing her hesitation, he asked, "Why do you not share my joy?" "I do," she answered but he knew differently. He said, "You have never lied to me before. Why do you lie to me now?" She told him of her facial condition, to which he replied, "I love you so much that I will stay blind. Your happiness means more to me than my sight."[2] His love for her was greater than a potential miracle of regained sight. That is sacrificial love.

Love is universal. There is no one on earth who does not need to be loved, some of whom are in extreme need of love. I read of a young man who was abandoned by his parents and brought up in an orphanage. He said that every so often people would arrive, and another child would be taken by the hand and led off down the road, accepted for adoption. His constant thought was, "What's wrong with me, why doesn't anybody love me?" He would press his nose against the window and watch as they walked out of sight, longing for someone to come for him. Then it happened. A nice lady came and took him by the hand and led him down the road. He was overjoyed. She became his mother. He felt so loved and, in essence, has never let go of her hand. An act of love provided a lifetime of joy for this young man.

I remember a visit I paid to an orphanage in Portugal about twenty-five years ago. Shortly after arriving, one little boy, maybe four or five years of age, came straight up to me and wanted me to pick him up. So, I did, and it was as though we were life-long friends. His face was beaming with a constant, infectious smile. The problem came when I went to put him down. He clung on with no intention of going down. I must have carried him around for an hour or so. Eventually a staff member had to extricate him from my arms. Such was his desire and need for attention and affection. Tragically, it is not only children in such a situation, today there are many adults who desperately need love and need to know they are loved.

Those Problem People

We all have run into those people who are very sullen and who really cannot be bothered to give us the time of day, even if they have a job that entails serving the public. I think of the person behind the service counter or the girl at the checkout in the supermarket, or the bus driver whose bus you catch to work each morning. These are people we think would be cheerful and engaging. On the day we encounter them, they are just the opposite

— uncommunicative, curt, maybe even rude. The temptation is to return like for like, to ask them if they got out of the wrong side of the bed. Instead, we need to be understanding. It is an opportunity to show love.

We have no idea what happened that morning in their life or even if there is an ongoing situation for which they are responsible, maybe a sick spouse or child. They could be waiting for some potentially bad medical news for themselves or a family member. Perhaps someone is dying in their family. They could be very disturbed by their financial plight. All these are possibilities of everyday issues that we all must deal with on occasions. It may not be easy, but why not attempt to find out what is so upsetting in their life at that moment? We need to offer compassion and let them know that someone cares.

I read where this very thing happened at a supermarket checkout, and through conversation an understanding lady discovered that it was the checkout lady's birthday and she had received no cards, no phone calls, not one person who had remembered her birthday. The scenario changed and it finished with the line of customers wishing her a wonderful birthday. It really made her day. So simple, yet so effective. We can make it our daily mission to spread understanding, love, and compassion as we go. It will make the world a better place. We can't change the world. I don't think we are called to do that, but we can make a difference in our own circle of friends and connections. Every act of love makes a difference.

The giving and receiving of love are critical for each of us. The benefit flows both ways. It's good to be loved but it is also very rewarding to give our love away. It might be a very simple act of coming alongside someone who is going through a medical investigation regarding a disturbing health symptom. They will feel our love as we show we care. Love is reciprocal. The more we give away, the more comes back to us. I love the quotation by Roy T. Bennett. He said, "Learn to light a candle in the darkest moment of someone's life. Be the light that helps them see; it is what gives life its deepest significance."[3] That's what love does as we reach out and love those who need it. But notice how he suggests that by doing so, it gives significance to the life of the giver. That's what happens. It's hard to give love away because it comes back in many other forms.

Somebody is wanting and waiting for your love.

CHAPTER FIVE

Love Thy Neighbour

We live in a world where there is so much anger, so much strife and animosity, which unfortunately, evolves into violence and conflict, both in and outside the home. It's probably a good thing that we are unaware of what might go on behind many closed doors. However, we are all aware of the grief and heartache brought about by the school shootings and other forms of murder. From the many notes left behind by shooters, we discover that they are mostly driven by hatred or revenge. So many people in our society today are hurting and need comfort. The world needs love. No question. But we are the world, so somehow, we are in the mix. So how do we fit in?

Obviously, we cannot be responsible for, and in fact can do very little about, the violence perpetrated around the world. We can only convey love in our small circle of family, friends, and colleagues, but that is all we are called to do, be a conveyor of understanding, love, and compassion. The ripples will go out from there.

How nice it is when you hear about some act of love between people. Rarely do you hear a story of love on the news, if ever. It's normally a diatribe of discord, conflicts, protests, opposing factions, and things that have gone wrong or are going wrong. The negative makes the news. Occasionally you may get a thirty second mention of something nice right at the tail end of the news, to lighten things up a little.

Even a display of collective love is heartwarming, like the young married teacher I learned about recently. She was pregnant with her first child, which sadly died in the womb at four months. Naturally, she was devastated. She was reluctant to go back to work, not knowing how she could handle the situation. But she went, only to find when she opened the classroom door, there on the wall were over a hundred paper butterflies with messages of love and encouragement. They carried such comments as "Remember, we love you," and "Don't give up on God." How lovely was that? In such a situation, the outward display of love gives strength, support, and encouragement.

The Greatest Commandment

Do you remember when Jesus was questioned as to what was the greatest commandment? His reply was, *Love the Lord your God with all your heart and with all your soul and with all your mind. This is the first and greatest commandment. And the second is like it: Love your neighbor as yourself* (Matthew 22:37-39 NIV). So, from the words of Jesus we learn that the expression of love within us must be upward and outward. It must first be expressed to God, and then to those around us. That is the calling of the followers of Jesus—love God and then love others. Love is often referred to as the most important of Christian virtues. Love is the basis for many other actions. Three readily come to mind—kindness, patience, and generosity. They are all motivated by love.

So, following the statement of Jesus, the immediate question asked was, "Who is my neighbour?" I suppose we could ask the same question today, considering that we supposedly live in a global village. It's interesting that within the response of Jesus it's assumed that one loves oneself when it says, *"Love your neighbor as yourself."* I think most of us love ourselves. But to love another equal to or as much as we love ourselves is no small task. Seemingly, we automatically love ourselves without giving it definitive thought, but extending that same consideration and love towards our neighbour is certainly not automatic. In fact, many years ago, C. W. Vanderbergh, in a sermon, offered a humorous line that may carry some truth. He said, "To love the world for me is no chore, my only real problem is my neighbour next door."[1]

Invitation to Joy

In answer to the question, "Who is my neighbour?" Jesus related the well-known story of a Jew who had been robbed and beaten and left to die at the side of the road. Several people saw him but did nothing for him, including other Jews. Then along came a Samaritan. Not only was this man a stranger but ethnically they were enemies, as the Jews normally would have nothing to do with the Samaritans. However, he tended to the man's wounds, put him on his own horse and took him to a hotel or hostel, where he could recover from his injuries. He even paid for his accommodation and promised to pay more if his stay was longer than arranged.

This man, a stranger, went far above and beyond what might have been expected even of another Jew. He showed compassion and generosity. He didn't think about himself, but he did what he knew to be right and not what was expected of him as a Samaritan. Then Jesus asked the question as to who the neighbour was. Obviously, it was the man who went out of his way to show love and who offered help to the hurting man. This was "loving your neighbour" in action.

In our English language, we only have one word for love. The language of the New Testament (Greek) has four words for love. There is *eros,* which is sensual love between humans. This is the derivative of the word "erotic." Then there is *storgé,* which expresses the love between family members. There is also *philia,* which carries the meaning of friendship and love between people. The same word would be used for love of your country. From this root, we get the word "philanthropy" and, of course, the well-known city of Philadelphia (which means the city of brotherly love). Finally, we have the word *agape,* which is demonstrated in God's love to us. It is a love that is selfless and unconditional. We see this love expressed to us through the sacrifice of Christ on the cross. This is divine love. It's a supernatural love.

This is real Christian love. It is Christ-like love. If we are followers of Christ, then this is the love that should be within us and the love we strive to give away to others. This is not natural love or human love. That kind of love tends to be emotionally based, self-centered and is often conditional. Christian love is different. It is a product of God's Holy Spirit and is therefore supernatural. It is an unusual love. It's an extraordinary love. It goes far beyond natural love. This is God loving others through us.

I read about a little boy who asked, "Where does love come from?" From what I understand from the story, he had never experienced real love in his life. How sad! The Bible helps us understand where love comes from when we read, *Let us love one another, for love comes from God* (1 John 4:7 NIV) and goes on to say, *God is love* (1 John 4:16 NIV). The very essence of God is love. So, love emanates from God.

As God is all loving and all forgiving, we are recipients of his grace and forgiveness because of his love. We are also told that he pours his love into our hearts so that we might share that love with others. Some situations in life are impossible to deal with without the aid of God's love in us. I think of those who lovingly work in the various slum areas of the world, giving sacrificially of themselves to literally lift people from the gutter.

Sometimes spiritual truths are hard to understand and this might be one of them, but God's love for us is totally unconditional, regardless of who we are, who we have become, and even what we have done. God knows us through and through, yet his love is the same. It does not depend on our action. We cannot earn it. It was St. Augustine who said, "God loves each of us as though there were only one of us to love."[2] What a great description of God's love and care for us.

Our response to his love is obedience to him and sharing that love with others. It is a deliberate act — we choose to love. As God loves us regardless of our condition, background, or culture, we are called to do the same. William Barclay, the Bible commentator, made a very interesting observation when he said, "More people have been brought into the church by the kindness of real Christian love than by all the theological arguments in the world."[3] Love is the practical outworking of the Christian faith.

You are probably aware of the passage of Scripture so often read at wedding ceremonies. It comes from 1 Corinthians 13 and reads as follows: *Love is patient, love is kind. It does not envy, it does not boast, it is not proud. It is not rude, it is not self-seeking, it is not easily angered, it keeps no records of wrongs. Love does not delight in evil but rejoices with the truth. It always protects, always trusts, always hopes, always perseveres.* This description of love seems so perfect. It's because it is the description of divine love. This is the love we aspire to have and seek to share.

This kind of love does not come with pre-conditions, it has no hidden agenda, is not self-centered and it does not demand power or position. It is patient and forgiving; it restores, it heals, and it unites. It is kind, humble, sensitive to others, acts responsibly, is compassionate, and generous, without expecting a return. If this kind of selfless love were more prevalent in the world, there would be far fewer broken relationships and broken marriages too. This love seeks to mend, to repair the brokenness of life. It reacts to nastiness with a kind spirit. It seeks to bring healing to a hurting person. In all situations, love is the response to the question, "What would Jesus do?" Our faith is expressed through love, and as our faith deepens, so our love develops and grows.

As followers of Jesus, we live throughout life guided by his words, *Love one another. As I have loved you so you must love one another* (John 13:34 NIV). This is our constant reminder to reach out to others. It's not our responsibility to change people but simply to love them as they are. In this world, we find a predominant response is to readily place blame, whether all the facts are known or not. It is so easy to sit in judgment rather than offer love. We can be quick to point the finger instead of offering understanding and forgiveness. We need always to be short on our fault-finding and long on our praise, short on criticism and suspicion and long on our acceptance and willingness to believe the best.

We need to give our love out freely and liberally. No one should have to qualify for it or earn it. Even when we just give someone our full attention and genuinely ask about their life and concerns, we are showing them love, that we care, and they are valued as a person and as a friend. So small and incidental but so important.

The expression of that love will differ according to the situation. Not all people need big hugs and a gigantic pat on the back. Some require just a quiet, reassuring hand on the arm and a genuine listening ear. Some are just looking for an empathetic response to show that someone cares and loves them. Mother Teresa once said, "It is easier to give a cup of rice to relieve hunger than to relieve the loneliness and pain of someone unloved."[4] Whatever form it takes, our love can touch a life and bring about a much-needed change. We may never know the depth to which our love has reached.

In considering the effect we could have on those around as we allow God to love others through us, I appreciate this quotation from *Good and Beautiful and Kind* by Rich Villodas, where, in talking about the love of God says, "His is the love that forms us to become the embodiment of wholeness for a world tragically fractured and breaking apart more every day."[5] This emphasizes for me the urgent need to be a vehicle of love to others and take whatever steps I can to make this world a better place.

Loving Your Enemies

It's not difficult to love those who love us. But what about those whom we perhaps dislike? Can we love people we don't know? What about those with whom we have nothing in common or those who have adopted principles of living we disapprove of? Is it possible to love everyone? What about people who believe differently from us? What about those with whom we disagree or those who deliberately oppose us? How should we treat them? How do you extend love to all? What about those who have hurt us? Most people would choose to ignore these kinds of people, but if you remember, Jesus went beyond telling us to love our neighbour; he said, *Love your enemies, and pray for those who persecute you* (Matthew 5:44 NIV). An impossibility, you say. Humanly speaking, I would tend to agree, but it can be achieved as we allow God to love others through us. Let me tell you an astounding story.

Invitation to Joy

We have a friend who was a pastor in a large Romanian church. He told us this story. He had a friend who was a well-known song and hymn-writer. His many songs are still sung in the churches of Romania today. During the years when the Communists ruled in Romania, this man suffered over seventeen years in a Romanian prison. Under the communistic ruling, the church and any associated with it were constantly subject to arrest and imprisonment. This man's crime was being a Christian and his apparent refusal to write songs for the Communist party. While in prison, he was subjected to constant torture. Every time he was tortured, he would say to the torturer, "God loves you, and I love you, and I hope to see you in heaven one day."

Shortly after the man was released from prison, this friend of ours had the occasion to visit him. The man opened the door with blood running down the side of his face. He said that his wound was the result of a visit from two secret police. Even after prison he was still persecuted.

Not many weeks later, there was another knock on this man's door. When he answered, he was very disturbed to see the chief torturer from the prison standing at the door. His immediate thought was that he had been sent to kill him. Apparently, this was their tactic, to send one man if there was to be a killing. Instead, the man said, "I have not come to harm you. Please, may I come in?" Once inside he uttered these incredible words, "I have come to ask your forgiveness. Your love has won me over." He went on to say that he too wanted the faith that this man had, and he wanted to be on the same side. They knelt together and prayed, forgiveness was granted, and they parted as brother to brother. A short time later the songwriter passed away.

Such love is difficult for us to comprehend. This was no normal love. It was an incredible example of supernatural love. This man was certainly fulfilling the command of Jesus to "love your enemies." Such love is possible only by the presence and power of God's Holy Spirit. It's true that few of us will ever have to face such suffering for our faith, but we are called to display such love. It's only divine love that gives us the ability to love the unlovely, and to love those who oppose us.

So, considering that story, it seems somewhat easier now to love our neighbours. But again, we could ask the same question, who are our neighbours? I would suggest anyone who crosses our path. They all need our love. Go and be the hands and feet of Jesus in a world that is desperate for love and compassion.

CHAPTER SIX

Nothing Is Too Small

Most people in the world can immediately recall what took place when they hear the numbers 9/11. The terrorist attack on the World Trade Centre in New York is burned into their minds. It seems that we all remember where we were when we heard about the hate-inspired terrorist attack that caused the horrendous death of so many people. However, another story that occurred at the same time is not quite so well known. It's the story of collective kindness carried out by the people of Gander, Newfoundland. Because the attack involved airplanes, all those in flight at that moment were instructed to land at the nearest airport. Thirty-eight unscheduled planes landed at Gander airport, in Newfoundland/Labrador, Canada.

The population of Gander is around 10,000 people. You can imagine the result of thirty-eight plane loads of people with 6,800 passengers and crew landing at a relatively small community. It was chaos, especially as it was unexpected, and no one had any idea how long they would be on the ground. It turned out to be several days. But the town totally lived up to the reputed Newfoundland friendliness. Schools and halls were opened to accommodate the stranded passengers. Local people opened their homes to take in people overnight. Others offered the use of their cars, cooked meals, provided blankets and pillows, baby food and other essentials required by so many people.

The kindness was recognized and appreciated by all. Some long-term friendships were established and the unplanned visit to Gander will be long remembered by, if nothing else, the selfless attitude and kindness offered to them.

Not only is the world in desperate need of love, but it also welcomes with open arms any act of love and consideration in the form of kindness. Through the Internet and social media, we have all become aware of random acts of kindness. There are hundreds of heartwarming stories where people have stepped up and acted selflessly, without fanfare, to help another person in trouble. It even makes us feel good when we read about them. It certainly carries much emotional benefit for the giver and the recipient. Such stories are worth reading just to lift the spirit. It's good to realize that whatever view we hold of humanity, there are still many people who will go out of their way to help their fellow travelers.

There is another story that is not so well known as the Gander story, but it has two sides to it. In November 1965, we here in Canada experienced a massive power outage that also covered the Northeast corner of the United States. I remember it well. It covered 80,000 square miles. An announcer on one New York radio station operating on emergency power was reported as saying, "An interesting drama is being unfolded on our streets. The price of candles in many stores has doubled. On the other hand, some kind-hearted merchants are offering their candles at half price and some even giving them away!" There we see the difference between selfishness and selflessness. One store took advantage of the situation while another acknowledged the plight of people and responded accordingly.

Being kind according to the dictionary is being friendly, generous, or showing benevolence. It often involves affection, warmth, gentleness, and a genuine concern for others. We also consider people to be kind by their manner, their attitude, their helpfulness, their empathy, and their understanding.

Kindness is an attitude that results in kind action. It can be the simple action of a smile, or the recognition of anyone who provides you with a service, such as a salesperson, a waiter, a police officer, or others with whom you have a passing contact. Telling people they are doing a good job, especially when their task appears to be so trivial or demeaning, is also an act of kindness. Have you ever told the lady cleaning the tables in the coffee shop what a good job she is doing?

Unexpected Kindness

There is a lovely story about Florello La Guardia, who was mayor of New York City many years ago. One day in 1935, he decided to give a judge from a poor part of the city the evening off. He then presided over the bench. The first case was an elderly woman accused of stealing bread. Asked whether she was guilty she replied, "I needed the bread, your Honor, to feed my grandchildren." He replied, "I have no option but to punish you. He fined her ten dollars but simultaneously put $10 into his hat and passed the hat round in the court. The lady paid her fine and in addition went home with $47.50.[1]

Encouragement is also an act of kindness. Appreciation and recognition are the desires of most people. Sincere praise is what motivates people to live up to the compliments paid to them. Encouragement does more to change a life than any lecture given on the need for change. There are very few people who do not need a word of encouragement, a pat on the back, a comment of appreciation for achievements accomplished. The power of praise is awesome. It is a kindness we can all practice. Compliment people today, because, as someone said, "They will not be able to read their tombstone."

The act of kindness certainly carries with it the ripple and the boomerang effect. George Skolsky, a motivational speaker, said, "Kindness is one thing you can't give away. It always comes back." The ripples carry the action further afield as the recipients of the kindness want to pass it on; but at the same time, there is a pleasantness and a feeling of satisfaction in oneself by the help and encouragement given. That is motivation enough for us to repeat the action. It's wonderful to be able to say, "I did the right thing. So, it cost me some time and a few dollars but what is that when looking at the big picture. I feel good about doing the right thing for someone who needed help." The homeless come to mind sitting outside the coffee shop, hoping for someone to buy them breakfast. Life's most persistent and urgent question, according to Martin Luther King Jr., is, "What are you doing for others?"[2]

Kindness is a matter of the will. One definition of kindness is doing what you can, where you can, with what you have. We should be willing to respond in kindness even when it is inconvenient, or perhaps even in situations with which we are not quite comfortable. Kindness means going the extra mile. J. R. R. Tolkien said, "Some believe it is only great power that can hold evil in check, but it is not what I have found. It is the small everyday deeds of ordinary folk that keep the darkness at bay by small acts of kindness and love."[3] How delightful it is to do something for someone who cannot repay you. Albert Schweitzer was of the same mind when he said, "Constant kindness can accomplish much. As the sun makes ice melt, kindness causes misunderstanding, mistrust, and hostility to evaporate."[4]

Empathy is closely linked to kindness. It is having the ability to come alongside someone and identify with them in their struggle. It's being able to get in their shoes and sense how they feel. To be able to share their pain, their disappointment, their grief, their sadness and even their emotional turmoil. Sometimes we need just to be present, to listen, and listen again, without trying to resolve the problem, but showing that we understand it. Often, few words are needed. Just to be there, in the moment, for as long as it takes. That's kindness.

Going Above and Beyond

About three years ago, a young man called Steve was found in a wooded area in the town of Wickford, where I came from in the U. K. Steve was in a bad way physically, having been beaten up by someone. He was homeless, cold, wet, hungry, and injured and had no one to help him. The man who found him, Duncan English, who was out walking, took him home, cleaned him up, and as they had no extra room in the house, he turned his garage into a bedroom for Steve.

When the story became known in the town, other people came forward wanting to help. It seemed to become a town-wide project, with much practical help being offered. An apartment was found for him, people contributed clothes and shoes as well as funds to help pay for rent and food. A local company even gave him a job. Can you imagine how he felt? That to me is kindness extraordinary. It was also a random act in response to a particular situation. Duncan could have just felt sorry for Steve and walked on, but instead he went out of his way to literally get him back on his feet and see him well again. He even recovered Steve's bicycle, which had been thrown into the river. This act of kindness reminds me of a quotation I read which stated, "A kind gesture can reach a wound that only compassion can heal." It was more than a kind gesture.

Humanly speaking, we are naturally concerned with our own problems and personal situations. Acting kindly sometimes requires ignoring our self-consciousness and perhaps our self-centeredness. Kindness often calls for us to overlook the inconvenience it may cause. We should try to put the other person's interest before our own at that moment. Normally, we don't do that. We are all busy people and have lives to run and families to care for. But if we want to be effective in helping others, we will quickly learn that it takes effort to deliberately choose to put someone else's need first.

Living with a consciousness to be kind requires us to be able to empathize with other people's situation and be ready in a practical way to meet their needs. If we always have kindness in mind, we will gradually become more sensitive to situations where we can help. It may be a very practical and physical need that can be readily met. On the other hand, it may be an emotional need that may require much understanding, patience, and even steer the person to get counselling, which may be the only solution. This is where we move away from a random act of kindness to reaching out to people we know who are struggling with life. This is empathy and kindness working hand in hand.

A true story is told in the United States about a young man dressed in torn jeans and wearing no shoes, who visited a particular church for the first time. The church was full. He walked to the front, assuming there would be somewhere to sit, but all the seats were taken. So, he chose to sit down on the carpet in the aisle. At once an elderly man got up from the back of the church and walked down the aisle to where the young man was. Some thought he was going to tell the young man he could not do that. Instead, the elderly gentleman sat down on the carpet next to the young man. What a wonderful gesture! He wanted to save the young man from embarrassment. He identified with him in his predicament. He showed understanding. What a superb example of love and kindness.[5]

We need no reminder that kindness to family and friends who are close should always be available and ongoing. They need to know we think about them, appreciate and care for them. Physical touch is also important, like a hand on the shoulder or a real hug. Occasionally, we will need to step outside our comfort zone, perhaps becoming vulnerable. Giving our undivided attention to someone who needs it is as great a kindness as any physical act of support.

Give Teenagers Their Due

Some teenagers are unjustly categorized as self-centered. Not so in this story. Many teenagers love their bicycles, I know I did. They tend to spend hours riding around. One young man was riding around the parking lot of a supermarket when he saw a man standing by his car with groceries in hand. He rode up to him and asked if anything was wrong. There was. The man had returned to his car only to find that he had locked his keys and his phone in the car. He said the spare key was with his wife at home, and as they only had one car, she could not bring the other key and he couldn't let her know anyway as his phone was in the car. Without hesitation, the young man gave his phone to the man and said, "Phone your wife and tell her that someone is coming to pick up the spare key." "But" replied the man "our home is a seven-mile round trip!" "Never mind that," said the young man. "I can do it." And off he went with directions in hand. Sure enough, one hour later he turned up with the key to the car. When the man wanted to know how he could compensate this good Samaritan, the answer came back, "No, not at all. I enjoyed the ride; besides I needed the exercise!"[6]

There are numerous stories of strangers stepping up with an act of kindness to fill a need and perhaps be the answer to someone's prayer. In some instances, kindness can be like an ointment on an injury. Mostly we will never know exactly how our actions have affected the recipient, but that matters not. We need not know.

Sophocles is thought to have said, "Kindness begets kindness." He was right because kindness is contagious. Even more significant is a quotation by Tolstoy, "Nothing can make our lives, or the lives of others, more beautiful than perpetual kindness." If a small kindness can make such a huge difference in a person's life, then we should have our radar set in looking to help someone today. There is joy in knowing you have made someone's life beautiful.

Just as a large fire can be ignited by a small spark, and as a mighty oak tree is produced from a small acorn, so a small act of kindness can develop into something much bigger and longer lasting than was originally planned. Here is a first-class example from six-year-old Bethany

Moultry from Georgia, U.S.A. Although very young, she saw a homeless man begging on the street. It upset her, and through tears she asked her mother if she could break open her piggy bank and give the man her money. Instead of that, she and her mother came up with the idea to distribute bags of daily essentials to homeless people. So, they co-founded Bethany's Happy Bags. I understand that at least 750 people in the Savannah, Georgia, area have been blessed by receiving one of these bags. Bethany says, "I help the homeless because I want them to know that there's someone out there who sees them and is thinking of them. It makes my heart happy to know that when they receive a Happy Bag from me, they know that someone sees them and cares."[7] Wise words from such a young person.

I recently read about the "hanging coffee" idea. This is where people pay for an extra coffee and leave it "hanging" so it is available for those who cannot afford it. Some places will accept payment for a similar arrangement with sandwiches or even a low-cost meal. Obviously homeless people learn where these places are and can request a coffee or sandwich. Apparently, the idea started in Naples and has spread around the world. A fantastic idea to spread a little kindness.

It was Harold Kushner, the American Rabbi, who said, "Do things for other people not because of who they are or what they do in return but because of who you are."[8]

Be someone who wants to make a difference in this world and in the lives of others.

How often have we heard it said about kindness, "If only there was more of this, the world would be a better place to live in?" I know I have said this several times, but isn't that what we all want, to make the world a better place? I am sure we all concur. We need to bless others with intent.

So, deliberately go out today and cause someone to have a glad heart. Even a smile can be kindness to those who need it. Surprise someone. Do something unexpected. It will go a long way to encourage and lift them up. It will lift you up also. Why not be the one to set off a wave of kindness, even better, a tsunami of kindness. Just a small act of kindness shows love and produces big results.

Be kind to a stranger. It will make their day.

CHAPTER SEVEN

Are We Ever Truly Contented?

Is satisfaction and contentment ever possible in this world of always wanting more?

Supposedly, John Rockefeller once received this question from a reporter: "Mr. Rockefeller, how much is enough?" to which he replied, "Just a little more." John Rockefeller was one of the world's richest men. His net worth in 1913 was estimated to be $900 million, which in today's dollars would amount to nearly $30 billion. Those four little words, "Just a little more," could well be the mantra of millions of people around the world. Have you ever thought that if only you had a little more, you would be better off and could manage more easily? The interesting aspect is that when we get a little more, a raise in salary or an increase in pension, it dissipates the same way as previously. We tend to live up to our income.

We live in a society that seems always to want more. Even rich people are not immune to the desire to acquire more wealth, although often it is just a desire to possess. I wonder how many people in the world are truly satisfied with their income. I also wonder how many people consider their income to be appropriate to the effort they expend in earning it. I have heard it said that either the employer is being exploited, or the employee is, dependent upon the level of wages paid. I am sure there is much truth to that: hence, the strikes and protests we see regarding income dissatisfaction.

Where does gratitude fit into our thinking? Gratitude is the result of understanding what we have and our privileged position in comparison to others. From my travels overseas, I have learned that we cannot see poverty and hungry people without being grateful for where we live and for what we have. I'm told that if we have a bank account and some money in our pocket, then we are among the world's top eight percent. If that is true, then we have every reason to be grateful for the situation we find ourselves in.

Gratitude means not taking things for granted, appreciating what we have, and not looking for things we don't own. Gratitude includes being thankful for the people in our lives, those who love and support us. It takes very little thought to realize just how many aspects of our lives call for gratitude. Let me give you one or two ideas. If you are reading this, then you are alive and can read, feel grateful. If you got up this morning and you could dress and feed yourself, feel grateful. If you are not sick, feel grateful. If you can experience and appreciate the beauty of nature, the blossoms and flowers in the spring and the trees coated in snow in the winter, feel grateful. If you have the love and support of family and friends, feel grateful. We could go on. I am sure you can recall many more scenarios in your life for which you are grateful or could be.

We should not need to have comparisons to cause us to be grateful, but allow me to share two little true stories that highlight the comparison between those of us who often take what is available to us for granted and others who do not have that luxury. A visitor to Canada from Africa was looking out of a window on to the backyard of the house where she was staying. She asked her host, "Who lives in the other place in the garden?" The host was mystified. The visitor then pointed out the large shed at the side of the lawn. "Oh, that is just a house for our car." The visitor was totally befuddled. She kept walking around and repeating, "A house for a car! A house for a car!" It was so hard for her to comprehend that not only do we have a house to live in, but we have houses for our cars as well.

I remember some thirty years ago we were hosting visitors from Eastern Europe. Having to pay a visit to a supermarket, I decided to take them along with me. Once inside, they abruptly stopped. They were shocked to see such vast displays of fruits and vegetables. Looking at all the produce they asked, "Is this all for sale?" Then they were even more blown away when they discovered a whole aisle just for pet food. It was beyond their comprehension. To discover that we buy food for our cats and dogs was astounding to them. Their animals ate whatever scraps they gave them or could find in the garbage. I have often thought of them when walking down the pet food aisle.

It is so easy to take our lives and what we own for granted as we are naturally engrossed in our everyday responsibilities. Gratitude helps to eliminate the thought that around the corner lies the next thing that will bring us satisfaction and happiness. It's sad that so many people waste their whole life concentrating on the arrival of the next thing in their lives and forget to live in the present. They look for the next salary increase, the next house, the next car, or another job, and so on, thinking that in them lies the secret of contentment.

The Benefits of Gratitude

The incredible benefits we derive from gratitude and contentment are enormous. Research has shown that those who practice gratitude are happier, suffer with less depression, are more positive in their approach to life, are more emotionally stable, and enjoy a calmer disposition.

A study of over one thousand people showed that those who had a grateful attitude benefited physically, psychologically, and socially. They had stronger immune systems, lower blood pressure, and slept better. They experienced higher levels of positive emotions, were more optimistic and expressed more joy and happiness. Socially, they were more outgoing, more compassionate and forgiving, and overall felt more connected, which resulted in a sense of less isolation. The daily practice of gratitude is known to reduce stress, and who does not need that?

Gratitude changes lives. I have been amazed to discover so many stories about people's lives being changed by their adoption of an attitude of gratefulness. People who have been slaves to addiction, homeless, hungry, unemployed, suffer mental illness and similar situations, have had their lives turned around and made full recoveries, solely due to their introduction to gratitude. It seems slightly incongruous to expect people in such disadvantaged positions to begin counting their blessings. But it worked for them. Most will tell you that it is only by the grace of God that they survived. We can learn much from someone who expresses gratefulness for one meal a day at a shelter or the person who is grateful that someone cares enough to get them medical help. Gratefulness eliminates bitterness and envy.

Practicing gratitude does not mean that we ignore problems or adverse events. We can retain a sense of gratitude by looking at the big picture of life, recognizing that the positives outweigh the negatives. It's difficult to be anxious and grateful at the same time. Even during adversity, gratefulness has benefits. When going through a dark patch in life, being aware of having had so much to be grateful for in the past, it's comforting to know that the blessings will return. It brings with it a sense of being cared for. For the Christian, this is when you know that God is the provider of all things, including the blessings of life. It is then that we have the sense that God is there caring for us through the rough times as well as the good.

Having a mindset of gratitude causes us even to wonder if we deserve what we have. It certainly eliminates the air of entitlement. Gratitude comes from the Latin word *gratia*, which means grace, graciousness, and gratefulness. It's a thankful expression of appreciation. So how can we express or display this gratefulness in life?

Some people start by looking back and seeing all the things in their life for which they should be thankful. They literally count their blessings. Then they look at the present and appreciate what they have now. Some think about and are grateful for people who have had a positive influence on them, both in the past and in the present. They write letters thanking them for their support and the contribution they have made to their lives. This proves to be a surprise and a blessing to those who receive such letters.

Other people keep a gratitude journal, where they record three, five, or ten things daily for which they are grateful that day. Each day they consider the privileges and advantages they enjoy and make their list. Some find it difficult at first and can only find one or two small, incidental things, but then as they become accustomed to the exercise, they begin to recognize more and more daily blessings in their lives as time goes by. By doing so, they create within themselves an attitude of gratitude that becomes an on-going blessing.

A gratitude journal has proven to be extremely beneficial psychologically. People who keep them tend to be happier, not so prone to depression, and adopt a more positive attitude. They also appear to have lower levels of envy and resentment. This whole exercise tends to be a great tool for encouragement, as they can check back regularly and be reminded of all those things and events that have been a blessing. It is often here that, in retrospect, they can see God's hand at work in their life. A prayer of thanksgiving is never out of place.

So, what's the result of this gratitude in our lives? Giving thanks certainly makes us happier. It lifts our spirit and creates a real sense of well-being. It affects our relationships with others. It tends to make us more aware of the needs of others and will instill within us the desire to reach out and do something about it. We will want others to enjoy what we are experiencing and be as blessed as we are.

Gratitude also creates contentment. In thanking a group of people for their assistance, St. Paul indicated that he had learned to be content in life, so whether hungry or having plenty to eat he was content. He illustrated the principle that gratefulness brings contentment. It even gives a great sense of peace and certainly makes our living more joyful. One of David Steindl-Rast's many quotations is appropriate: "The root of joy is gratefulness . . . It is not joy that makes us grateful: it is gratitude that makes us joyful."[1]

Make every day Thanksgiving Day!

CHAPTER EIGHT

Can We Afford Not to Give?

When a fourteen-year-old boy in the United States learned that his mother had been diagnosed with breast cancer, and knowing that his parents would have trouble finding the money for medical treatment, he wanted to do something about it. He came up with the idea that he could go door to door with a small pair of clippers and offer the neighbors the opportunity to snip off some of his hair for a small donation. He asked his father if he thought $100 was a good target. His father agreed but cautioned him not to be too optimistic. The boy went out with clippers in hand. He returned later, totally bald, but with $1,225.00 in his hand. His generosity was the sacrifice of his hair and the giving of himself to help his parents financially.[1] A commendable feat.

There is a distinct close link between kindness, gratefulness, and generosity. Gratitude invariably will lead to generosity, and by generosity we are not necessarily talking about money. It is an emotional expression of a heart full of thankfulness with a desire to share with others the blessings we have received and enjoy. When we appreciate and are grateful for what we have, we inevitably want others to share in our sense of good fortune. When we give to others, we feel closer to them and they to us. This is one of the benefits of opening our hearts and hands to meet the needs of others.

Generosity comes in many different packages. When the word comes to mind, we automatically think of money, but that is only one aspect. We can be generous with our time, with our possessions, with our energy, or perhaps with our support for a colleague. Giving time and attention to a sick relative or friend is being generous. Hospitality can also be an expression of generosity. This is where kindness and generosity overlap. Generosity is selflessly giving to others for their benefit while expecting nothing in return.

The Amount Is Not Important

You may remember that Jesus once watched people putting money into the temple offering box. A widow gave two copper coins and he said that she gave more than others, because they gave out of their wealth, but she gave out of her poverty. There is no measurement of generosity. Although donations are usually made from our financial ability to give, that is not always so. Sacrificial giving often means going and giving beyond that level. One person might give a large amount while someone else gives a much smaller amount, yet the smaller amount might have been a greater sacrifice.

In referring to monetary gifts, we need to give quietly, even silently, without fanfare. It should be unconditional, not expecting anything in return. The Bible says, *When you give to the needy, do not let your left hand know what your right hand is doing* (Matthew 6:3 NIV), which simply means keeping a low profile of our gift. Sometimes the recipient need not even know where their help came from. When we give, we don't need to look for recompense, or reward, or praise. Just enjoy the deep satisfaction of helping someone in need. Brian Tracey, the well-known motivational speaker, once said, "Always give without remembering and always receive without forgetting."[2]

Charles Spurgeon, the well-known minister of Metropolitan Tabernacle in London, in the mid-to-late 1800s, and his wife, were criticized and thought stingy because they sold the eggs their chickens laid. People thought they should give them away. However, when Mrs. Spurgeon died, it came to light that all the money they collected from selling those eggs was given to two widows. Others may not know how much you give or understand where you give and why you give. That matters not. We must always follow our heart and give where we desire to help. God sees and knows and that is all that matters.

Giving to others in need brings satisfaction beyond happiness. There is a deep-down feeling of having done something essential, helpful, and valuable. What we give may be small to us but could be very large to those who receive it. We may have caused a positive change in their situation but may also have changed their belief that someone cares for them. I know I quote Mother Teresa often, but she made some very pertinent statements during her life. On giving, she said, "It's not how much we give but how much love we put into it,"[3] which highlights that our motive is more important than the size of the gift. You can be poor but generous. In fact, it has been noted that often poor people are among the most generous. Although for most of us, we are all richer than we think. Generosity is not measured by the size of a bank account.

Winston Churchill once said, "We make a living by what we get. We make a life by what we give."[4] That statement could not be more applicable than to a man named Robert G. Letourneau from the USA. He lived from 1888 to 1969, so he saw two world wars and lived and worked through the depression of the early thirties. He held several different jobs in the engineering trade until he was asked by a landowner to level 160 acres. That was when he discovered that the machinery available was quite inadequate for the job. So, he built his own machine and went on to become known as the inventor of earthmoving machinery.

He started his business around the beginning of the depression, but despite that, it flourished. Even when he had little money or was in debt, he insisted on giving away 10% of his income, the traditional tithe. As time went on and his income grew, he began giving away a greater and greater percentage, 20, 30, 40, 50%. Eventually, for many years before he died, he was giving away 90% of his income and living on 10%. He became a well-known philanthropist and donated funds to commence a university in Texas. He worked on the principle that you cannot outgive God. It seemed that the more he gave away the more God gave back to him.[5]

I believe that God has put a law of reciprocity in place, which is the boomerang effect. Your giving is always returned to a greater degree than your sacrifice. The Scriptures indicate that if we give to the poor, we are lending to God, who repays us accordingly.

Keep to Your Promise

Commitment is also important. If we make a commitment to give, whether financial, physical, or material, we must keep to what we promise. My wife and I made a commitment to financially support someone in their work on the mission field. We let things slip because of very, very tight financial circumstances. It was Rita who reminded me that we had not kept up our commitment.

It may seem foolhardy now, but I wrote a cheque with nothing in our bank account. By the time the cheque passed through the bank, there were funds in there to cover it. We were working on a commission-only sales position then. Once we decided that the commitment should come first, sales came in and our finances improved immediately.

Research shows that generosity can have a beneficial effect physically and mentally. Just like being kind, giving can reduce stress and even depression. Apparently, psychologists have discovered that giving to others activates the area of the brain associated with contentment, inferring that generosity makes us happier and creates a sense of wellbeing. The researchers are probably right, but I certainly concur that by helping others you help yourself. In fact, the more we act charitably, the more we find we want to do it. It seems to be self-motivating.

There is no shortage of needs in the world, from individual people we personally know who need help, to organizations that do a first-class job of bringing relief and healing to those hurting. They all need our support. But sadly, there is also another side to this. We occasionally suffer from compassion fatigue. That occurs when we see so much poverty portrayed on our television screens that it no longer fazes us. We simply change the channel. On the opposite side to that, we can also feel quite disturbed, even guilty, or at least extremely conscious of the fact that we have plenty to eat while others are starving.

But what do we do when our heart says one thing and our pocketbook says another? I usually go with my heart but with wisdom. We must always be wise and sensible. So many good causes may tug at our heart's strings, but discernment must come into play. It is always a balance between head and heart and fulfilling our sense of responsibility. We are all called to be good stewards of what God has entrusted to us; however, I think in the end we never lose by giving. Anne Frank is quoted as saying, "No one ever became poor by giving." Giving is love in action.

Often a spirit of generosity shows up when someone appeals for help. I remember the appeal in the U. K. on behalf of a little boy named Oscar Saxelby-Lee. At age four he was diagnosed with an aggressive form of cancer of the blood. A public appeal was made for potential stem cell donors to be tested to see if their blood or DNA matched this small boy. Incredibly, in his hometown of Worcester, England, 4855 people lined up in the rain to be tested. The attitude among the volunteers was, "It is the least we can do!" Through crowd funding, hundreds of thousands of dollars were raised to send Oscar to Singapore for specialized treatment. It was successful, and Oscar was declared cancer-free in October 2020. His mother Olivia said, "He's gone from being told he might never walk again to running around like any normal eight-year-old-boy."[6]

It was an outstanding act of generosity for so many people to be willing to stand in the rain to have their blood tested for a little boy they never knew. It was yet another act of kindness and generosity for people to donate funds to get little Oscar the treatment he needed, especially considering that he was a stranger to most of the donors.

There is no doubt that we are richer than we think. I quoted in an earlier chapter, if we have a bank account and some change in our pockets, then we are among the world's top richest eight percent. If that is so, then ninety-two percent of the world's population are below us financially—a daunting thought. Generosity is being selfless and kind, reaching out to alleviate the needs of others. It is also an expression of empathy and love. Amy Carmichael is quoted as saying, "You can give without loving but you cannot love without giving." Giving helps to move our focus away from ourselves and on to the needs of others. If we give thoughtfully and intentionally into a specific situation, we cannot help but experience happiness and joy in knowing we have made a difference in someone's life. Isn't that what we are called to do?

If you give of yourself out of a heart of gratitude, surprisingly you will find there will always be plenty more to give.

CHAPTER NINE

Attitude Is Everything

I have a friend who loves helping people. In fact, he suggests that we are here for that very purpose and I think he's right. He talks to everyone and makes them feel important. He will do anything he can to provide for people in need. He says, "If it is within my ability to help, I will," and he does, even taking people to where they need to go in his vehicle. I guess we would call him a people person. He enjoys serving others. His attitude is commendable. Albert Schweitzer had a similar thought when he said, "The only ones among you who will be really happy are those who will have sought and found how to serve."

Attitude is one of the most important aspects of our lives. Our attitude makes a huge contribution to an enjoyable life. Our attitude to the circumstances of life creates our experience of life. It most often means the difference between living life to the fullest or just existing. Earl

Nightingale, a motivational speaker, said, "Attitude is the reflection of the person inside."[1] We share our attitude with the world without saying a word. Our body language often says it for us. A shrug of the shoulders, the rolling of the eyes, a dismissal wave of the hand, a purposeful ignoring of a comment, all convey our feelings and attitude.

Our attitude to life, to people, to work, to family, to friends, and especially to ourselves, is critical. All these aspects give or take away from enjoying a pleasant disposition. Adopting a positive attitude to life enables us to achieve things that may surprise us. It is said that people who believe they can't do something are usually right and so are those who believe they can. It is all in the attitude. Attitude is that strong. It will trigger a positive response in the mind and body to achieve what needs to be done. Having ability means being able to achieve something, but how well we do it will be determined by our attitude.

Attitude Is Our Reflection

We may not think too much about it, but all situations that bring us in touch with people are affected by it. What people see on the outside indicates to them who we are on the inside and how we feel. Attitude says it all. How do we come across to people? Do we have a critical spirit, or do we have a pleasant and accepting attitude? Do we portray ourselves as judgmental or do we show an encouraging spirit? Do we have a jealous streak in us?

Do we look enviously at what others have, always thinking we have been left out or left behind, always wishing things were different, never satisfied with what we have, always thinking there is more or should be more? If we do, then we are displaying an attitude that is of no help to ourselves or others.

A common phrase is, "attitude is everything," and I understand why that is said. Our attitude colours our thinking and influences our perceptions. We may think we perceive the world around us as others do, but in fact we all have our own perception of reality. Our understanding of reality hinges much on the preconditions set by our attitude, which has been shaped by our experience. Every aspect of our lives is affected by the attitude we carry within us. People we meet respond to us according to the attitude we portray to them. If we are positive and upbeat in social settings, then we will mostly get that treatment in return.

The opposite is also true. If we face the world with a negative and depressed demeanor, others will reflect that back to us or will avoid us altogether. It affects how we see the world, how we see other people, and how we interpret events and situations. We will either see the world in an optimistic and agreeable manner, or we will see everything with pessimistic eyes and find life generally disagreeable.

I read recently about two young ladies working in a community hospital who had decided to quit their jobs because they had had enough from patients and co-workers. They considered patients to be ungrateful and full of complaints, their co-workers to be disagreeable with backbiting, and the administration to be apathetic. Before they left, they decided to try an experiment. They would bend over backwards to be nice to people. So, they overwhelmed people with encouragement, courtesy, and appreciation. Suddenly, they discovered everything had changed. The patients no longer seemed so miserable, their co-workers were smiling at them, and the administration appeared to show an interest in their affairs. Nothing had changed except their attitude and now everything appeared to have changed.[2] We have no control over circumstances, but we do have control over how we react to them.

Comparisons Rarely Help

Do we have an attitude of comparing ourselves to others? This is a common practice, but it's one we should readily drop because of our unique differences. We all come from different backgrounds, upbringing, schooling, and have different occupations. Our DNA and fingerprints are uniquely different. Our life's journey has been different from each other. We look different, think differently, act differently, hold different views on life, and have unique preferences. It makes no sense to compare ourselves with others.

Comparisons are pointless. In fact, it has been said that "comparison is the thief of joy." Not one of us has travelled the same road. Because of our differences, we make and have made different choices. Those choices led to different lifestyles, different roads, different careers, and hence, different achievements. If we want to make any comparison, we should be doing it with ourselves. How do we stack up today as opposed to yesterday?

When we struggle financially, it's not uncommon to wish that we had what others have and that our life would run as smoothly as theirs. However, we are looking only on the outside. We have no idea how smooth or rough their life really is. We see the lovely house and the nice car. We think of them as a well-groomed family with good jobs and likely a good income. We see them as having it altogether and life appears wonderful. But we have no idea of what is happening inside. They may have internal hidden pain, or they might be suffering extraordinary discord in relationships. They could well be struggling to keep everything looking good to the outside world. Our envy, or dare I say jealousy, may be totally misplaced. The probability is that we are only causing ourselves unnecessary angst, and that never improves our own situation. It really is a matter of attitude.

How much healthier and better for us and others if we display an attitude of kindness and generosity. We need to ignore what others appear to have and seem to be enjoying and concentrate on displaying an attitude of optimism and positivity. If we show a spirit of appreciation and gratefulness, others around us will benefit. It tends to be contagious and spreads like ripples on a pond. If we act as though we got out on the wrong side of the bed or like the proverbial bear with a sore head, how can people warm up to us? We need to be people whom others enjoy being around. We need to be those who can lift the spirits of other people by just being with them. We benefit as much as others when we convey a positive and congenial attitude.

In one of my previous books, *Discover Your Hidden Self,* I shared the story of Anton Chekov, the famous Russian writer. His father was a tyrant. He, his four brothers and his sister, all suffered abuse at the hands of their father. The father acted under the guise that God wanted him to beat them to keep them humble. The abuse caused two of his sons to move far away from their village to Moscow.

The father owned a small shop in the village, but because of his constant drunken state it went downhill economically. Chased by creditors, the father went and joined his two sons in Moscow. The mother tried to carry on, but the business became bankrupt, so she too took two more sons and her daughter and moved to Moscow also. Anton stayed in the same place, studying for three years and all that time blaming his father for their family's diabolic and disastrous experience.

However, after living with that bitterness and resentment for three years, he had a change of mind. He came to learn that his father was beaten as a child and was acting out what he had suffered. Abuse was normal to him. Suddenly Anton had an overwhelming love for his parents, including his father. He joined them in Moscow, found them all living in a one-room basement suite, took charge of the situation, and helped all of them with education, jobs, and a new place to live. What had happened? Nothing had changed, yet everything had changed. The only thing that had taken place was that Anton had seen his father in a different light, changed his mind and changed his attitude. The whole family benefited from one son changing his attitude.

The same thing can happen today. Most often we are unaware of what other people are going through or the position they find themselves in. People tend to hide their adverse situations. How often do we make judgment calls and assume things that turn out to be incorrect? We see only the exterior. We make assumptions without having all the facts. We all have obstacles, difficulties, struggles, and brick walls to face. Our attitude to them will determine our disposition.

Attitude is mentioned in the Bible, where we are encouraged to take on the attitude of Jesus who, throughout his earthly ministry, was humble, compassionate, and loving to all he met. His attitude to the poor, the sick, and the disadvantaged was nothing but exemplary. We would do well—in fact, we could do no better—than to follow his example. His attitude was that of a servant. If we are his followers, we can do no less.

Have you ever enjoyed the interesting pastime of sitting and watching people as they walk by? Some smile, some nod, while others simply ignore you as though you are not there. Some appear to be very serious. It's hard to tell from facial expressions what their face might be hiding. We don't know the battle they might be fighting in their life at that moment. They could be struggling with all kinds of personal or relational issues. They could be on their way to work knowing that they are going to lose their job. They could be on the way to the hospital to see a loved one who is dangerously ill. We have no idea.

It's true, we may all be facing different issues, but our needs are the same. We all want to be loved, accepted, and understood. Knowing this should encourage us to display to each other an attitude of kindness, love, and understanding. Life really is a matter of attitude. If we have control over our minds—which we do—then we have control over our attitudes. It's something we determine. Most people know us by our attitude. Hopefully, it's an attitude to be admired and one by which we want to be known.

CHAPTER TEN

The Comfort of Forgiveness

To lose a child to death is devastating, but to have your child murdered must be one of the most tragic and heart-breaking events a parent could face. In 1992, Amy Biehl was brutally murdered by four young black men in South Africa. Her home was in California, but she was in South Africa on a scholarship to work with the anti-apartheid movement. A young black boy had been killed by police and tensions were running high. Unfortunately, Amy was seen as representative of the white opposition, and despite protestations from black friends, she was stabbed and stoned to death. Amy was there to help change people's lives for the better. She was trying to help rid the townships of poverty and squalor. She was there only to befriend, to help, and to change lives.

Her parents, Linda, and Peter Biehl, were naturally devastated in losing their daughter, but after reading

Amy's diaries, they were motivated and inspired to derive something positive from her sacrifice. They established a foundation in her name to continue her work. Linda and Peter went to South Africa to meet the people with whom their daughter had been working. They organized development projects there for the benefit of the locals. People were trained and employed in welding, sewing, printing, and baking. They founded a construction company, built sports facilities, and introduced adult literacy programs.[1]

Bishop Desmond Tutu had established a Truth and Reconciliation Commission that provided the opportunity for reconciliation between the opposing sides of apartheid and attempted to turn hatred into love. The Biehls wanted to be part of that by offering forgiveness to Amy's killers. That opportunity occurred in a practical manner, when unexpectedly they came face to face with two of their daughter's killers. It was not easy. Real forgiveness is never easy — it takes choice, willpower, and determination.

It was to their utter surprise that two men, Easy Nofomela and Ntobeko Peni, turned up at their foundation after being released from prison. They wanted to help promote the work of the Foundation. Linda and Peter Biehl admired these two men for having the courage to face them and offer to work with them. They stayed and worked for many years, during which time the Biehls and they established a wonderful relationship. Nobeko shared, "I don't know how they found it in their hearts to forgive us, but I can tell you it has greatly enriched my life. I will never forget the kindness they have shown me when they had every reason to hate me." From Linda Biehl's side she said, "Forgiveness is really about liberating yourself, letting go, so you can be rid of hate and bitterness. It's a one-way street that doesn't need the other person to do anything . . . Reconciliation is a different step. It's really hard work." By offering forgiveness, the Biehls released themselves from an imprisonment of bitterness and positively affected many other lives in doing so.

Obviously, that was an outstanding example of forgiveness not faced by many, but few people, if any, can get through life without the need to give or receive forgiveness. Rare is the person who can live without disagreements with others. As humans, we are prone to making mistakes. It's not difficult to step out of line, to do something to cause another person disappointment or hurt. It's often unintentional, even done inadvertently, and sometimes unknowingly. Unfortunately, innocent misunderstandings can lead to damaged relationships. It seems that conflict is part of being human.

Forgiveness Is Powerful

It's not difficult to link joy with forgiveness, although the road to forgiveness can be rather bumpy. Forgiveness has one of the most powerful effects upon our human psyche, both from the giving and receiving of it. To give it is to be released from a prison of anger and resentment. To receive it is to be released from underlying animosity and guilt for being the cause of the rift.

It's common knowledge now that several illnesses are mind-related; in other words, our mental activity has a direct relation to our physical conditions. It has been discovered that high blood pressure, heart attacks, anxiety, depression, stomach problems, headaches, and sleeplessness can often be traced back to the experience of unforgiveness, from the stress, resentment, and bitterness it causes. The colon seems to be a favourite place in the body for reacting to stress and worry. Guilt increases the heart rate and blood pressure, both of which have an adverse effect upon the cardiovascular system. A lack of forgiveness is also known to have an adverse effect upon mental health.

Forgiveness, on the other hand, can have a positive effect upon our physical conditions. By withholding forgiveness, we do more damage to ourselves than the person who is waiting for forgiveness. The person who caused us the hurt can do no more than ask for forgiveness, and then can move on with life, while we continue to hang onto the hurt and live with the resulting resentment and sense of animosity.

Nelson Mandela was held for 27 years as a political prisoner; that is a very long time! He deliberately forgave those who put him there. He acknowledged that hatred and bitterness are destructive but that there is power in love and forgiveness. He is reported to have said, "Resentment is like drinking poison and then hoping it will kill your enemies."[2] We allow others to continue to hurt us while we hold on to anger, resentment, and bitterness caused by their action. When we let go and forgive, we are released from a self-imposed prison. It is we who gain freedom, peace, and serenity. The weight is lifted. We feel free. While we hold on to these negative feelings, we do ourselves great emotional and physical disservice.

James E. Faust, an American religious leader, lawyer, and politician once said, "If we can find forgiveness in our hearts for those who have caused us hurt and injury, we will rise to a higher level of self-esteem and well-being." Forgiveness does not change the past, but it certainly makes a difference to the future.

Few of us have not experienced hurt. The pain of unwarranted criticism is very real. It pulls you down, even when you know the accusations are untrue. I know from personal experience the pain of being wrongly accused in public of a misdemeanor that never occurred. The desire to put it right or strike back is overwhelming. I always believe that truth surfaces in time, as it did on this occasion. Most of us have experienced the results of wrongdoing. Either we have been the recipients of it, or somehow, we may have been the cause of it. It usually results in relationships being severely damaged. Fortunately, forgiveness has the power to heal the hurt and restore relationships.

On a much lighter note, disagreements can be created quite unintentionally. We might simply see a situation differently from someone else. We feel strongly about it and are reluctant to compromise or change our thinking or position. We hold our ground because we firmly believe we are right, as does the other person. Rather than agreeing to differ and keep the peace, we allow a situation to arise which only produces harsh words, resulting in damaging a perfectly good relationship. Unfortunately, both parties leave disillusioned and nursing a hurt that only forgiveness from both sides will heal.

In those situations, we must ask ourselves what is more important, that we be right, or that we not damage a good relationship. Sadly, these unresolved situations can continue for months or even years. The only resolution is whatever it takes to bring about reconciliation and a repaired relationship, which is usually the olive branch of forgiveness.

How sad it is when you hear that siblings have not talked together for years because of some disagreement, or parents have ignored their children because something was done to upset them. It's tragic when families are split apart over differences of opinion, or misunderstandings, perhaps separated for years, all possibly carrying resentment and bitterness. Some drift apart and even totally lose contact. This is not how families were meant to be.

The ability to forgive comes from the power of love. Love has the power to overcome the hardest of situations. If we take an honest look at our hurts, they probably pale into insignificance if compared to the atrocities that have occurred against others. As mentioned earlier, when we read of parents who have forgiven those who have murdered their child, we are astounded and find it difficult to understand. We wonder how that could be done. In such a situation, we ask who benefits. It is always those who offer forgiveness, those who let go of the hurt. They are released from their incessant pain. I refer to this extreme and extraordinary act of forgiveness as it gives us a comparison that demonstrates how our hurts tend to be of a much lesser nature and can more easily be put to rights.

I personally know of a family where a young man killed his own grandmother on his mother's side. I cannot comprehend the mental anguish and turmoil of his mother having her mother murdered by her own son. I have no idea how she dealt with such a situation. Again, I am sure it makes our hurts, although very real and painful to us, quite small in comparison.

None of us is perfect. In recognizing that, we should exercise grace and not expect others to be perfect. Hence, in our state of imperfection, we make mistakes. We fail to keep promises. We cause disappointment by our action or non-action. We are known to let each other down. We make judgment calls that turn out to be incorrect. Sometimes we fail to keep up with the standard that others have come to expect of us. Intentionally or unintentionally, we say things that are hurtful.

In all these situations, we find ourselves standing in need of forgiveness. We resist apologizing because we think we are right. Pride makes us think we must defend our ill-advised actions or our victimhood. Can we really expect forgiveness if we are unwilling to grant others forgiveness? Again, pride can be a real hindrance to our offering forgiveness. It takes two to repair and rebuild a relationship. The good aspect about it is, when a relationship is repaired and rebuilt, the new relationship is often stronger after the act of forgiveness, even if the healing takes time.

In many situations, it would be a good thing to step back and take time to process what has taken place. Then forgiveness can be given at its proper time. Then it can be done thoughtfully and from a proper perspective. The act of forgiveness is that important. It needs to be done right.

We make the decision to forgive with our mind, but true forgiveness comes from the heart. It comes from a heart of love and compassion, both of which help in the forgiveness and healing process. In fact, our love determines our willingness to forgive.

The pain from physical and sexual abuse is beyond description. Its effects are devastating and can last for years, and sometimes a lifetime. Forgiveness in cases of abuse does not come easily. In fact, it is probably the most difficult of all wrongdoing situations to deal with. Many abusers were themselves abused, although that does not make it right or justify such behaviour. It does, however, bring an element of understanding, and perhaps creates one step towards forgiveness. I honestly believe that it's only by the grace of God and through the love of God that forgiveness can be genuinely offered in such situations. Much time is also needed for healing, and counseling is often essential.

How do we forgive when we suffer emotional hurt from the actions of another person, whether intentional or not? How do we overcome the enormous disappointment when we lose trust in someone? The sense of rejection is devastating. We have no choice but to face it. Recognize it for what it is. Recognize the suffering it is causing and then consciously make the decision to forgive.

When we forgive, we choose to forgive. It is an act of the will. However, our act of forgiving is not an act of accepting, excusing, or condoning the behaviour that caused the hurt. In fact, it could be said that it is an act of self-protection because we choose to let go of the hurt and release ourselves from further suffering. It is we who benefit the most when we forgive. It takes strength and courage to forgive, but the result is always worth the discipline. It just takes one person to act humbly and make the move towards resolving the issue.

Forgiving Oneself

The act of forgiving oneself appears to be much harder than forgiving someone else. We seem to be able to play down mistakes by others more than our own. Being human brings with it the ability to do wrong, to step out of line, to do or say the wrong thing, sometimes with unexpectedly adverse results. How often have we wished to go back in time and take back the things we said thoughtlessly or carelessly? Unfortunately, we cannot turn the clock back and we are left to deal with the situation as it is.

Then there are times we might reach the point of wanting to say "sorry" to unburden ourselves of the mistake we made, only to find that the other person has moved away or passed on, and now that opportunity is no longer available. How do we deal with that? I believe it can be resolved. Some people have become so overwhelmed with guilt and the need to give or receive forgiveness that they have gone to extreme lengths to find the person concerned to put things right – even travelling great distances to be able to experience forgiveness face to face. If that is not available, we can still genuinely offer forgiveness from our heart and mind. Even if their address is unknown, we can still write a letter to the person who is grieved. Writing it out tangibly is a practical act of remorse. We can then be free to forgive ourselves and move on with life. The letter put away in a drawer is always a reminder that you have played your part and sought forgiveness.

As already noted, to forgive oneself is not easy. It is far easier to continue carrying the blame for the mistake you made, especially if your actions have affected your own family. It means coming to the place where you recognize that you are not perfect and that your actions were not a deliberate act to hurt or injure.

To begin the process, we need to accept responsibility for what happened. That does not mean we rationalize what we did to justify our actions to make them acceptable. That is skirting around the issue. It means admitting what we did was wrong and wanting to put it right. We need to express genuine remorse and take steps to apologize and make things right with those we may have hurt. That's the biggest hurdle. It takes courage, but it is the way forward.

Once we have done that, we can forgive ourselves. We must show understanding, kindness, and compassion to ourselves. Feeling guilty about what we did is normal, but by taking positive steps to heal ourselves and the other party, there is no need for shame. From that point on we don't dwell on the negative aspects or feelings from the past but learn from the experience and move on, determined to do better, and avoid the same mistake again.

Self-forgiveness is necessary for good mental health. It will help to remove the potential danger of anxiety and depression. Our self-image and our sense of well-being will immediately improve. We will feel the burden lifted, be lighter in our spirit and will feel better overall about ourselves.

Forgiveness and God

A few years ago, a friend asked me to visit a lady in hospital. When I arrived there, I found a very distressed lady. Knowing she had not long to live, she was extremely disturbed because she was uncertain that God had forgiven her or even would forgive her. I spent some time with her, prayed with her three times—at her request—until finally she moved from being uncertain to being assured that God loved her, and that she had his forgiveness. At the time, I wondered just how many other people might be suffering the same mental turmoil, unsure of God's forgiveness.

Forgiveness from God is central to the message of the Christian faith. Jesus referred to forgiveness on many occasions in his three-year ministry on earth. He was once asked how many times we should forgive, should it be up to seven times? His reply was, "seventy-seven times," which indicated not a specific number, but that we should forgive endlessly. He emphasized that we should be liberal with our forgiveness so that we in turn may receive forgiveness.

Regardless of religious persuasion, many people know what is commonly called the Lord's Prayer. Included in it is this sentence, "And forgive us our debts as we have also forgiven our debtors." Do you notice those two little words "as we"? We are asking God to forgive us as we—in the same way and to the same extent—are willing to forgive others. That puts us on the spot regarding our forgiveness toward others. Knowing and experiencing God's forgiveness produces immense peace and joy.

Why do we need God's forgiveness? Have you ever noticed that none of us had to be taught to do wrong? We appear to have an inbuilt capacity and ability for wrongdoing. As children, we had a natural tendency to go that way, to be self-centered, maybe selfish and want, or perhaps even demand, our own way. As adults, it seems we are no different. We are all aware of our secret thoughts and sins, our inability to exercise self-control. That's because we are all born with a nature that is at variance with God. We inherited that state and with it a condemnation, which is why we feel we need to be forgiven. But God is good, loving, and kind, and freely offers forgiveness to remove that barrier between us and him. The good thing is that we can be forgiven and enjoy a close relationship with God. We can be assured of his forgiveness. It is only a prayer away. We will return to this subject later, as it is important for each one of us.

Summing Up

Forgiveness is no easy call. It's very hard at times to give or receive forgiveness. However, for the sake of our mental and physical health, we must learn to do just that. To heal that broken friendship, that fractured relationship, takes just one person to act humbly and make the move toward resolution.

The American author H. Jackson Brown Jr. said, "Never forget the three powerful resources you always have available to you—love, prayer and forgiveness." Forgiveness is not a sign of weakness or capitulation; it is a sign of strength. It takes strength and determination to forgive and to move on.

Some would say to forget the past. It has gone forever. I would say, if you can, set the past right first, then you can let it go. You will be more at peace than just ignoring it and hoping it will go away. The experience of being forgiven is superb. If you need forgiveness, ask for it. If you need to forgive, then offer it; you will be glad you did. It will be like enjoying a fresh breeze on a hot summer day.

CHAPTER ELEVEN

No Time to Say Goodbye

Once a friend of mine asked me out for coffee. He said he had something important to tell me. It was a shock. He told me the doctors had given him eleven to twelve months to live (not sure how they can be so precise). Twelve days later my friend was dead. He had no time to say "goodbye." Suddenly, he was gone. The uncertainty and brevity of life is always with us. I once read, "Do not regret growing old. It is a privilege denied to many."

We are not promised tomorrow. We have friends who took a trip to visit their son and his family. They had a wonderful time. Arriving home, the next day, they received the devastating news that their son had died of a heart attack that morning. He was 49. Death is not reserved for the elderly.

This is not meant to be morbid but a simple consideration of the trail we leave behind. Are you planning to leave a legacy? Many of us don't have much of a financial legacy to leave, but that is not as important as other forms of a legacy. Think about this question, "How will they remember you?" The "they" can be anyone—family, friends, colleagues, and acquaintances. We will all leave something, some influence or even just memories. But what will those memories be like?

Most of us would love to have been in line for a legacy. Even if that was not to be, I am sure we all wish we could leave our families a legacy. I did see a bumper sticker, however, which said, "Live long enough to spend your children's inheritance." You have probably also heard the humorous story regarding the astuteness of a woman whose husband was tightfisted with his money throughout his life and wanted to take it with him when he died. He made his wife promise to put his money with him in the coffin and bury it with him. To this she agreed. So, when he died, she dutifully wrote a cheque and placed it in the coffin.

We will leave all that aside because here we are not talking about a financial legacy. We are talking about the legacy of memories and influence. I believe we would all like to leave a mark on the wall of life to say, "I was here." It would be good to say, "This is what I contributed to life, and this is what I am leaving behind." What is probably even more important is this, "How will your children remember you?" Some of us have few memories of our grandparents, but we do have memories of our parents. Our children are closest to us and know us best. Once we are gone what memories of us will they cherish?

What will spring to our children's minds every time they think of us? Hopefully, it will not be a crusty old cantankerous individual who was always difficult to please. That is the opposite to what I would wish. Rather, I would like the memory to be one of a person who has shown consideration and understanding and has had a loving disposition toward family and friends. The life we live now is contributing toward that memory.

We all will leave a legacy of ourselves. We have no choice. Although I know nothing about John Nichols or his book *The Nirvana Blues*, I discovered an excellent quotation on legacy from the book. He wrote, "Each person leaves a legacy, a single, small piece of himself, which makes richer each individual life and the collective life of humanity as a whole."[1] An excellent observation. I am sure our desire would be to leave something of ourselves that makes others richer because we were here. A wise thing to remember is that the things we do for ourselves die with us; the things we do for others live on as part of our legacy.

A Well-Lived Life

It is said that a good legacy is a well-lived life, but what does that mean? I am sure there are many different answers to that question. In our retirement community,

Invitation to Joy

we have met some very well-travelled people who have seen and done many things that would certainly register as lives well lived. Others would consider that rising to a prestigious position of power and influence is also such a life. Achievement and success in various fields of endeavor would probably also qualify for such a description. Then, of course, there is always the acquirement of wealth and possessions and the freedom and trappings they may bring.

I am sure all these aspects contribute to what might be called a full and satisfied life, and there is nothing wrong with any of them. I would just ask the question as to what is left behind to say the person was here and the difference they made for being here. I come back to the critical question embedded within this book when I ask myself, "Have I made the world around me a better place because of my being here?"

At birth, we all arrive with nothing. When we finish life's journey, we are equal because we leave with nothing. So, what takes place in between is important, since it relates to the trail we leave behind. There used to be a popular saying, "He who finishes with the most toys, wins." I don't agree with that because all the toys are left behind; but what do they say? "I acquired and owned all these." So what? Do they bring lasting, happy memories for family and friends left behind? Personally, I question myself with, "What have I done that others will know I passed this way?" I would love to be able to say with St. Paul, "I have fought a good fight. I have finished the race. I have kept the faith."

Who we are is far more important and is a richer legacy than any possessions we might leave behind. What I might have achieved will not be remembered more than the example I tried to set. Our children and grandchildren will hopefully be reminded more of our love and kindness to them, perhaps our faith and other aspects of us, as opposed to any material legacy. The attitude we display and the life principles by which we live will hopefully be embedded within their memories.

Have you ever considered writing a letter of blessing to your children? In such a letter, you describe to your child what they have meant to you and your appreciation for them. Maybe recall some special moments that you remember. They may be surprised but they will treasure such a letter. One friend went further, she wrote down their life story for their children and grandchildren. There are probably many people who wished their parents had done the same. There were lots of questions I wished I had asked before my own parents passed away.

We may have little money, but we can still leave a rich inheritance. We can leave a positive influence by investing our time, our energy, and our efforts into the lives of people now. Showing love, respect, kindness, and support to family and those around us will indicate how much you care for them. That will always be remembered. Instead of leaving a mark on the wall of life, leave an indelible mark on the life of a person, an indelible legacy that cannot be compared to anything financial.

Mario Raul de Morais Andrade was a Brazilian poet and novelist. He once wrote about the value of life and what he wanted to experience in his time left on earth. He likened it to a little boy with a packet of sweets. At first, he ate the sweets with relish and pleasure, but when he realized there were only a few left he began to enjoy them intensely. He didn't intend to waste any of the leftover sweets. At the end of the piece, he wrote these meaningful words, "We have two lives and the second begins when you realize you only have one."[2] He died at the age of 51.

It's good to remind ourselves that this day will never come again. We have all heard it many times, but it's true. All we have is the present. We must live in the now as we are not promised tomorrow, although, what we do today will count for tomorrow if there is one. Life now is the real thing. Life doesn't give us a re-run. Hence, our decisions are critical for us and for others around us. We have heard the common phrase, "Life is what you make it." So, let's make it good, enjoyable, and worth living.

I have discovered that one of the main things that haunts people as they come to the close of their life is regret. Regrets of things said, things not said, things done, things not done, and even what they might have achieved or who they may have become. If you are still on the right side of your funeral, then you still have time to make changes and put some things right or put them in place. It's worth giving it some thought.

So, there we have it. Life is short. Our time is limited. We have only one life. We need to make it count. We need to work at living a life now that reflects honorable principles where others come first. Live to be missed. Live a life by which you want to be remembered. That way your legacy will be invaluable and unsurpassed to those left behind. Let's live a life that outlives us!

CHAPTER TWELVE

When Things Go Wrong – And They Do

Many people in North America will recognize the name Dave Dravecky. He was an all-star baseball pitcher who played in two National League championships and one World Series game. He began his career in 1982 but it was cut short in 1989 after he lost his left arm to cancer. Dravecky was devastated. He suffered with depression and other stresses and tensions brought about by the amputation. However, his courage and resolve, along with his faith in God, brought him through. He said, "I've come to understand that God is really shaping and molding my character. I've come to realize that real growth of character takes place in the valleys of life." His was a deep valley. It took him a while to climb out of it.

We live in a world where bad things happen to good people. As part of humanity and living in a fallen world, none of us can avoid adversity. Jordan Petersen, in his book *12 Rules for Life*, says, "Because we are vulnerable and mortal, pain and anxiety are an integral part of human existence."[1] I am certain we all concur with that thinking. All of us experience the adverse effects of anxiety, sickness, pain, grief, ageing, and the inevitability of death. We have no in-built protection from these issues. We are all vulnerable to life's unforgiving blows.

Just as an aside here, allow me to say this. When things go wrong, and they do, don't ever give in to the temptation to blame yourself. It's true that sometimes we make mistakes—we are not infallible—but blaming yourself for something that may have been out of your control is only damaging to your self-image and self-esteem. Even if a decision you made has seemingly come back to bite you, remember that you made the decision in good faith with the knowledge you had at the time. Your self-worth is determined by who you are on the inside, not by any external event or occurrence. Keep up a positive attitude and a good self-perception to help you face life's darker moments.

Few families can avoid the scourge of cancer. We probably all know family members or friends who have battled this insidious disease for many months, only to succumb to it in the end. Others live with pain. My wife, Rita, has suffered the increasing debilitating effects of Parkinson's for over fifteen years. We have friends who lovingly care for their spouses as they suffer the ignominious stages of dementia. Even everyday stress can produce adverse medical conditions. These things seem to be the daily uphill battle that most of us face.

We may well consider our adverse situations to be intolerable but think for a moment of someone like Dr. Henry Viscardi from New York, who was born without legs. He spent his first seven years in charity wards of various hospitals with people being unkind and without understanding his unfortunate predicament. For many years, his stumps were encased in padded boots. Until a miracle happened. His doctor, Robert Yanover, was determined to help him and had a set of artificial legs made for him. It changed his life. He eventually married and had four children.

Until he died in 2003 at the age of 91, he dedicated himself to assisting people like himself. In his life's work, he helped thousands of armless and legless veterans adjust to life and accept themselves. He brought them more than limbs; he gave them purpose and hope for a meaningful life. He became known as the "Voice of the Disabled." Out of his adversity many others were blessed.[2]

Maybe your world has recently been rocked by some nasty occurrence. Perhaps someone close to you has been diagnosed with a serious medical condition. Perhaps a family member has passed away and you are feeling the hurting void left in your life. Maybe your marriage is a little rocky just now. Perhaps your son or daughter has been bullied or abused at school or worse, been in an accident. Maybe it's something quite different, such as your finances being in a mess, your job security being precarious, or your search for a job seemingly hopeless. We could go on. It is at times like these that you begin to think that life is just too overwhelming. Adversity seems to strike us all at some point in our lives and it's not easy to deal with.

No Way Out

At times, we feel pressed in from every side with no visible way out. We get hurt and things grow emotionally painful. Relationships are torn apart. You wonder if healing will ever come. So much depends upon how we see and respond to life's obstacles. We have no choice. They come our way, they block our path, and it's difficult to find a way around them. They bring fear, trepidation, confusion, and a sense of helplessness. They might even bring about depression and anger. But in the end, although difficult, we are forced to face up to them. Thus, our attitude and approach in handling these situations will help us through the unwanted experience. But how do we do that?

First, we must honestly take stock of the situation. Look at where we are, where we want to be, and what it is that we are facing. Usually nothing is insurmountable. J. Sidlow Baxter, in his book *Awake, My Heart*, says, "What is the difference between an obstacle and adversity? Our attitude toward it. Every opportunity has a difficulty, and every difficulty has an opportunity. If the best things are not immediately possible then immediately make the best of the things that are possible."³ Helen Keller, who was the first deaf and blind person in the USA to earn a college degree, said, "A happy life consists not in the absence, but in the mastery, of hardships."⁴

In 1979, fifty-two Americans were taken hostage by Iranian militants. It turned out that they were ultimately held captive for over a year. During that time, there was an American military attempt to rescue them. Sadly, it went horribly wrong and was unsuccessful. It was not until a change in the Iranian government, and the economic results of sanctions, that they were released in January 1981.

Among those held hostage was Gerry Earl Lee, age 37, married with children. He indicated it was a terrifying time made worse by solitary confinement and the Iranians putting on mock trials and inferring the sentence of death. He said, "I thought I was dead." Then he felt a miracle happen. His captors allowed him to have a Bible, much to his surprise. While reading, he came upon Isaiah 43:5, where he read, *Do not be afraid, for I am with you, I will bring your children from the east and gather you from the west.* He told his father when he arrived home, "When I read those words, I felt God was making me a promise. Somehow, I knew I would reach home safely. The whole experience became a lot easier after that."[5]

What a comforting and strengthening experience that must have been for him. While away in prison, his wife and family also suffered terrible mental anguish at home, not knowing how he was and what would happen to him. What a joyous occasion for them when he returned home.

For Gerry Lee, this was an extreme case of adversity, and fortunately, few of us will ever have to face such a situation. Reading about Gerry Lee and his ordeal in prison, I wondered what might be learned from his action. He was in trouble, so he took steps to invoke God's intervention. He read God's Word, the Bible. He received a specific text from Scripture that he felt applied to his situation. He believed the text was for him and he trusted God implicitly to fulfil the promise, which he did. We need to follow his example. If we get such a portion of Scripture that applies to us, then we also need to hold on to it, and trust God to fulfill his promise in our life, to bring us through our adverse situation.

I think it's safe to say that our adversities are likely to be far less than imprisonment, but they are very real to us. Suffering cannot be categorized. Suffering is suffering. Pain is pain. Grief is grief. Each of us might handle our situation differently, but it makes it no less painful, disturbing, and perhaps even devastating. We react in different ways to similar adverse conditions. But there are no easy answers. No suffering is light or easy; in fact, it is hard. Difficult as it may seem, we are forced at some point to look away from the present and look ahead to see that there is a future. That is not minimizing the present suffering or any situation, but simply trying to encourage the lifting of our eyes away from the hurt and on something that may begin to bring healing.

As we go through life, we discover that circumstances and situations don't always work out for us as we planned or hoped, but this is where our faith comes in. If we believe that God has our best interest at heart, then we must take our hands off the situation and allow him to work things out. That is what the Scriptures teach. Look at Romans 8:28, where it says, *And we know that in all things God works for the good of those who love him...* Because God's love is constant, permanent, and unchanging, he is working things out for us even when, and if, we are unaware of it. We certainly do not always understand why we are having to go through the adverse situation we find ourselves in. At times, we think God is distant or even absent, but he continues to work things out behind the scenes. It is often only as we look back that we see God's love demonstrated for us.

This may seem a strange consideration, but we should be grateful for tears. We are emotional beings and God has given us the ability to cry. We experience tears of joy, tears of laughter, but also tears of grief, tears from pain, and other aspects of suffering, and even the tears from a broken heart. Man or woman, there is no shame in crying. Crying is a safety valve. Crying is good and necessary. Tears bring release and relief. Tears often begin the process of healing.

It may seem incongruous to think that we are talking about joy and adversity at the same time. They may seem a contradiction in terms, but believe it or not, many people attest that, for them, joy came out of adversity. I am reminded of a flight I took when the weather was overcast with heavy rain, but within a few minutes after taking off we broke through the clouds into glorious sunshine. It reminded me that the sun is always shining, even if we cannot see it. After we have experienced the rain, how much more pleasant is the sunshine. How appreciative we are of the serenity of a lake after experiencing a storm. So it is with life. How wonderful it is when the hurt, fear, the pain, and unpleasantness of life's storms move on, and we enter a state of peace and calm. For some people adversity has been a blessing in disguise.

I have already referred to Helen Keller. What a superb example of overcoming her circumstances. She was deaf, speechless, and blind from early childhood. Yet she went on to be recognized for her greatness and contribution to the world. She shared, "The marvelous richness of human experience would lose something of rewarding joy if there were not limitations to overcome. The hilltop hour would not be half so wonderful if there were no dark valleys to traverse."[6] Several writers have pointed out that it's only in the darkness that we see the beauty of the stars.

Grief is painful, regardless of age. A friend, Jon Jay Vincent, was very young when he lost his father. On the fiftieth anniversary of his father's death, he wrote some poignant words. He said, "The world I knew was ripped apart. At the time, it was terrible. Years later, it was still painful. I would never be the same. My father, my daddy, my world was gone. My mother's world changed too. But what could a boy of eight do? I could hear her cry every night and I cried too. The door was closed but, a door, a bedroom wall, nor the dark of the night could muffle her midnight tears and her soft cries. It was a terrible time. I can't tell you the depth of that loss and the financial struggles it brought. Poverty was not far from the front door. My sadness rolled into anger and anger into bitterness. All was lost for me the day my daddy died. But then one glorious day amid my bitterness, a hand from heaven reached into a little boy's heart and introduced me to my heavenly Father." Jon indicated that he had felt totally lost, but now he had been found. A new joy was his. He never stopped missing his father, but his solace from grief was found in a relationship with God, his heavenly Father.

In one of my earlier books, *Miracles: Coincidence or Divine Intervention,* I wrote about another friend who suffered many years before succumbing to cancer. He would talk about the downside of losing control. He disliked having to rely upon doctors, nurses, relatives, and friends for everything. He found it to be very disconcerting. However, in contemplating his situation, he wrote the following words: "Whenever I feel panic, fear or depression, it is often a sign that I am counting on my own limited and undependable resources or at least on other insufficient and unreliable resources, rather than on God. I need to learn how to disengage this 'auto-response' or 'default mode' which seeks refuge, solace, or solutions solely in my own resources. I need to train my heart into the habit of turning to God in dependence and trust, no matter what comes my way. God alone is my ultimate resource and my refuge of absolute security. That's where I want to be." Thought-provoking words. Excellent sentiment and a wonderfully expressed desire.

Let Down and Abandoned

Adversity hits in different ways, for one person it's illness, for another it's being abandoned. I recently read about a lady called Sue Richards. Let me tell you about her. Eight years into their marriage, and having just relocated to another city, her husband walked out on her, leaving her four months pregnant and with a two-year-old son. She was devastated. She felt abandoned, unloved, rejected, and extremely vulnerable. She now had no house, no job, no husband, and no church connection, just a little boy who continued to ask heart-breaking questions. Living in temporary accommodation, she struggled carrying a toddler and groceries up three flights of stairs while pregnant. Every night she sobbed into her pillow. But she prayed and prayed constantly.

Then, she says, from deep inside came the knowledge and assurance that God still loved her. The promise of God became very real when he says, *Never will I leave you, never will I forsake you.* (Hebrews 13:5 NIV). Things did not turn to glitter overnight, but in her loneliness and sense of abandonment she held onto those words and trusted that God would keep his promise. She indicates that he did and gave her the daily strength to see her through this bitter life-changing experience.[7]

Christian or not, whether it is desertion, divorce, or death, the pain is the same. Losing a loved one causes grief beyond description. Even if there is some comfort in knowing that they are in a better place, have lost their physical sickness and infirmities, and that eventually we will be reunited with them, there is still the aching void. Some have likened it to being in a fog, and it's not until that fog begins to clear that the real world comes back into focus and then the relief begins. In other adverse situations, like illness or broken relationships, the hurt can be just as debilitating. Even being hit by joblessness or an accident, the stress and anxiety are identical. There is no easy answer to suffering and adversity. However, I believe the Christian has resources to help overcome adversity.

The first resource is seeking God's intervention in prayer. Prayer itself strengthens, but answered prayer provides an enormous spiritual and emotional lift. Corrie ten Boom was imprisoned by the Nazis during the second world war. She writes, "Prayer is such an important power. In the concentration camp, seven hundred of us lived in a room built for two hundred people. We were dirty, nervous, and tense. One day a horrible fight broke out amongst the prisoners. Betsie (her sister) began to pray aloud. It was as if a storm laid down, until at last all was quiet. Then Betsie said, 'Thank you Father.' A tired old woman was used by the Lord to save the situation for seven hundred fellow prisoners through her prayers."[8]

When you bring God into the equation, things change. If we did not believe and know from experience that God listens and answers prayers, our faith would be in vain. However, we have seen so many "coincidences" in our lives which confirm that God is at work behind the scenes for those who pray.

At our lowest point, there is only one way to look, that is up—to God. In times of bereavement, we experience an overwhelming sense of loss. It leaves us feeling empty and lonely. It hurts. Life seemingly will never be the same again. The Psalmist felt the same way when in Psalm 116 he says, *The cords of death entangled me, the anguish of the grave came upon me; I was overcome by trouble and sorrow* (NIV). But then he goes on to describe his next move. He says, *Then I called on the name of the Lord: 'O Lord, save me!'* Why did he do this? Because, he explains, *The Lord is gracious and righteous; our God is full of compassion.* He describes the result. God brought him comfort and healing.

Even if we have a strong faith, it does not preclude us from pain and suffering. That comes with being human. C. S. Lewis, in writing about pain, said, "Pain insists upon being attended to. God whispers to us in our pleasures, speaks to us in our consciences, but shouts to us in our pain. It is his megaphone to rouse a deaf world."[9]

At our darkest point, we need to turn to the Light, which is God. In his incarceration, we saw that Gerry Lee turned to the Word of God, the Bible, and found a word of encouragement from God. He trusted God and his faith was rewarded. Sue Richards did the same. She found a promise in Scripture that God would never forsake her. She held on to that promise and things turned around for her. Whatever dark valley we are going through, we can present our situation to God in prayer and seek his intervention. In fact, the Bible encourages us to do just that. It says, *Cast all your anxieties on him because he cares for you.* (1 Peter 5:7 NIV) It may be that we need simply to ask for strength or comfort to get through the situation or even get through the day. God is sovereign and he can change things if he so chooses.

God can heal our illnesses if that is in his will to do so. Invariably, we find that, like St. Paul, God's grace is sufficient to help us overcome our difficult time. In our weakness, we can know God's strength. St. Paul asked God three times to heal him, but he discovered that God doesn't always heal, even when asked, but he always has a purpose in not doing so. For Paul, it was so he would know and experience God's grace and strength in his own weakness. Fanny Crosby, the well-known song and hymn writer, lived for eighty-eight years totally blind. She was only six weeks old when, being treated for eye inflammation, something went terribly wrong, and she was left totally blind. Yet later in life she maintained a belief that her blindness was a gift from God. She considered it aided in her prolific songwriting career. She wrote more than eight thousand over her lifetime.

Dietrich Bonhoeffer, a theologian who was imprisoned and ultimately put to death by the Nazis just a month or so before the end of the Second World War, wrote these words, "God does not give us everything we want, but he does fulfill His promises leading us along the best and straightest paths to himself."[10]

If everything in life were perfect, we would never learn anything. Just as the plant must push its way up through the earth, and in doing so become strong, in the same way adverse aspects of life tend to make us stronger. As mentioned earlier, adversity really can be a blessing in disguise. The blacksmith puts the iron through the furnace, hammers it into shape, then thrusts it into ice water. The result is an instrument that is strong and ready for use. Someone said, "That which doesn't break us, builds us." We may get battered by the storms of life, but they will not destroy us. Faith faces the storms and wins. Fortunately, storms do not last forever.

It may seem strange to suggest we count it as a joyful occurrence when we go through struggles and trials, but that is what the apostle James says in his epistle (James 1:2.) J. B. Phillips translates it like this: *When all kinds of trials crowd into your lives, my brothers, don't resent them as intruders, but welcome them as friends! Realize that they have come to test your endurance. But let the process go on until that endurance is fully developed, and you will find you have become men and women of mature character. . .*

It's true that we may not have a perfect life. We may not have all our ducks in a row, as the saying goes. Things are not always neatly in place, but we recognize that, for many of us, life is never as bad as it could be. Over the fifteen years dealing with my wife's Parkinson's, when we go through a particularly difficult patch, we remind ourselves that there is always someone worse off than we are. At least we still have each other, and many others would like to be able to say and experience that. We have learned that God is with us even if we feel knocked down. It is he who lifts us up again because he loves, he cares, and he wants us back on our feet.

Let me conclude with a slightly humorous quotation from Mother Teresa. She said, "I know God will not give me anything I can't handle. I just wish that He didn't trust me so much."[11] Maybe you feel the same. Remember, God always has his purpose.

CHAPTER THIRTEEN

That Elusive Purpose

Life is but a blink of the eye, a flicker of the eyelid. Yet most of us would like to know that we passed through this moment with purpose. There is joy in knowing that we have lived a purposeful life. As I have said before, we like to think that we were here for a reason, and that while here we achieved something, or at least that the world knew we were here by the mark we made. Mark Twain said, "The two important days in your life are the day you were born and the day you find out why."[1]

It's sad to hear that there are people who just drift along quite aimlessly with little purpose, who seemingly just exist as opposed to living. Even more sad is to hear of those who consider their life futile. However, I recognize that some want it that way and are quite happy in that situation. The potential life offers each of us is phenomenal. Yet many of us experience but a small portion of that potential. Sometimes it's because we were not looking for it or ready for the opportunity. In this connection, Winston Churchill made a most relevant statement. He said, "There comes in the lifetime of every man that special moment when he is figuratively tapped on the shoulder and offered the chance to do a very special thing, unique to him and fitted to his talent. What a tragedy if that moment finds him unprepared for the work, which could be his finest hour."[2]

A 32-year-old bankrupt man stood on the shores of Lake Michigan on a cold winter's night, contemplating suicide. Looking up at the stars, the thought came to his mind, "Do I have the right to end my life?" The answer to himself was, "No! I have no right to eliminate myself." He suddenly felt overwhelmingly responsible for his life. He turned his back on the lake and set out for home with the purpose of doing something good with his life. He certainly accomplished that. His name was R. Buckminster Fuller, who became a world-renowned engineer, mathematician, architect, and inventor. He owned 170 different patents by the time of his natural death many years later.[3] Purpose gave him a reason for living and led him to the fulfilment of his potential.

A common reason we may miss our potential in life is that certain questions remain unasked or unanswered, such as, "Why am I here?' or "What is it I want to achieve?" or "How best can I use my life?" However, I believe that these questions belong to a discussion of long-term purpose. The objective here is not to talk about our life passion of what we would like to achieve—there are plenty of books on that subject—but what happens in our everyday life and how purposeful it is or might it be.

Most people want an enjoyable life, a life that is pleasant and pleasurable, but many of us want more than just enjoyment and the pursuit of pleasure. If we are honest, we would admit that we want more than just happiness, we would like to enjoy a life of peace and joy. We look for a meaningful or purposeful life. We would like to know that we are achieving something in life, more than just passing through, that our lives have some significance, that we are contributing to society to bring about change and making a difference in the world.

Here's the crux. Adopting an attitude of wanting to make a difference in the lives of others and doing something about it leads us to a purpose-filled life. Knowing that we are achieving something significant and doing something special brings satisfaction, contentment, and a sense of purpose. Our life is counting for something.

We all have everyday purposes that relate to our responsibilities within our families and elsewhere. These I call on the surface primary purposes, but I believe we can experience a deeper, overall purpose in life, to give reason for being here, something that displays our usefulness in life. I think we need to seek a purpose that is beyond ourselves, something that is outside of our everyday activity. I believe the secret is in touching the lives of others in need. I think this adds meaning to our lives and provides inner satisfaction and happiness.

Having a purpose creates motivation and direction, especially when it will benefit others. Our actions are determined by our purpose. The action itself is not the purpose. The desire to help is the purpose. An interesting study of hospital workers revealed that, when told the benefits of handwashing, not to themselves but to the patients, they were 45% more likely to wash their hands more than normal. In other words, the purpose motivated their actions even when the result was not a direct benefit for themselves but to protect the health of their patients.

Age Makes No Difference

Even children can have a vision or purpose and can achieve much with their young lives. I think of a young man named Ryan Hreljac.[4] In 1998, at the age of six, he heard that children in Africa were dying for lack of clean water. He wanted to do something about it, so he started doing chores around the house to get enough money to have a drinking well built in Africa. In one year, he raised enough money to build his first well. It was at a primary school in Uganda. However, once started, he inspired others to join him. Eventually, with the help of his parents, he developed a website for the same purpose. A newspaper story was written about him in 2010, and at that time his efforts had been rewarded by the building of 602 wells and other sanitation plants, providing clean water for 685,000 people. He set out with the purpose to save children who were dying in Africa from polluted water. He certainly did that and more.

In *Discover Your Hidden Self*, I wrote about an eleven-year-old girl named Jessica Rees who was suffering from a brain tumor but who desperately wanted to do something to brighten the day of other children in the same hospital. She began by giving away her own collection of beanie babies in brown paper bags with stickers on. Her father obtained some plastic containers, and they began to fill them with toys and goodies. They became known as Joy-Jars, after Jessica's second name. What Jessica started at a local hospital spread across the United States and ultimately to 27 countries. Although Jessica succumbed to her illness, it is impossible to know how many children around the world were blessed because she, one little girl, set out with the purpose of cheering up other children in the same plight. Anyone can have a similar purpose. It is recognizing a need and stepping up to the plate to take care of it.

As you see, we are not talking about a total life purpose, as in something you want to achieve with your whole life, like becoming an engineer, a concert pianist, or a medical specialist. These are overall and long-term goals. Here we are referring to what may be a short-term purpose, but effective, nonetheless. If we get up in the morning and deliberately look to see what we can do to make a positive change in someone's life, then we have a purpose. Benjamin Franklin used to think first thing in the morning, "What good can I do today?" and at the end of the day, "What good have I done today?"

Does Our Purpose Change?

As the years go by, our everyday primary purpose changes. My purpose today is far from the purpose I had thirty years ago. Then it was being a good husband, a good father, and using my ability and strength to help others, as I worked for a mission in Eastern Europe. Today, my primary purpose is caring for my wife. That is my full-time calling. However, that does not nullify the purpose I carry of wanting to help and serve others daily. These purposes work simultaneously. Primary purposes and sub-primary purposes work together in our lives, just as we have short-term focus and long-term vision. Some might justifiably say, "Caring for my family," or "Keeping bread on the table" is my primary purpose, and that would be right, but having a secondary purpose of reaching out to others adds something special to your daily routine.

As I indicated earlier in the book, because I look at life through the eyes of a Christian, I must consider what is the purpose of a person with faith. Let me share with you my understanding on that.

Having faith in God and a relationship with him provides its own purpose. As we have already seen, Jesus said the first and greatest commandment is to love your God with all your heart, soul, and mind. That is the first part of any Christian's purpose in life, to love God. The second is this. As followers of Jesus, we are called to display his characteristics and follow his example and do what he did in reaching out to those around him who needed love and compassion—the very essence of what is being encouraged in this book. The Christian's desire and delight is to serve God. That is the very purpose for which God calls us into a relationship with him. If we are believers, then our actions are motivated by our love for God and his love for us, as well as fulfilling the purpose of serving him. Following in the footsteps of Jesus is a high calling. It is a divine purpose that is a privilege to carry out.

To be a blessing to other people and to leave the world a better place is an admirable purpose. We can all have that as our goal, and in doing so it will create a purpose-filled life. Our faith in God predetermines our goal and calling. For the Christian, his or her actions are determined by the purpose of serving God. We serve him by serving others.

Finding a purpose in life is the subject of many books. Why is that? It's because deep down significance is important to us. We want to know that our lives here have had some meaning and that we have not been a non-entity or just another number among the world's eight billion people. We are all significant in our own way, especially to our families and to those around us, but it is important to each of us that inwardly we have a sense of purpose as well.

I would encourage you to take a little time and look back at the path you have travelled. Take note of the places where only you could have achieved what was accomplished. You were uniquely placed where it was possible for only you to show the love and support needed at that time. Friends, relatives and even strangers have crossed your path at specific times, and you alone were able to meet their needs. It proved that you were in the right place at the right time. It was no coincidence, it was God-ordained timing.

Allow your mind to go back and remember what others have said to you. Maybe they have made comments about your kindness, thoughtfulness, wisdom or expressed appreciation for your help and support. It is worth noting what other people say because they tend to make spontaneous objective observations.

You probably have a larger purpose in life than you could possibly imagine. I believe too many people put themselves down as having accomplished very little, whereas if they look and think a little deeper, it may surprise them just how much they have achieved and contributed to life along the way. So be encouraged. Lift your head up, put a spring into your step and realize that the world is a better place for you having been here.

So, if someone came along today and put you on the spot by asking you, "What is your purpose?" What would your answer be?

CHAPTER FOURTEEN

Where Do We Go from Here?

When we finish reading a book, most of us want to feel it was worth the time invested and want to enjoy a feeling of satisfaction from having done so. With fiction, it's satisfying if the story ends well, even if it was different from what we expected. If it's non-fiction, then we want to feel we have learned something to take away, something that has been informative and helpful or at least something to which we could relate. As the purpose of this book was for me to help steer you toward joyful living, I trust that by encouraging the activity of loving, giving, and serving, it has highlighted a basis for enjoyable living. Hopefully, it has shown a pathway to having a real purpose in life.

Perhaps you know of situations where you can be the Good Samaritan, or your heart is telling you to do something similar of a practical nature; then I would encourage you to listen to your heart. Many people have lived with regrets because they did not listen to their heart and mind. If you feel the urge to reach out to someone, to be kind to them, to be generous, to show love, to build a relationship, then it would be wise to do so. Give action to your thoughts. You will not regret it because of the boomerang effect I wrote about earlier. What you do will always come back to reward you. Happiness and joy are among the rewards.

Joy and Happiness

The subject of joy is not thought about very much. Happiness is far more prevalent on people's minds. However, there is a distinct difference between joy and happiness. We all want to be happy, and most people would say they are. However, if you ask about joy, then there is some ambiguity, some haziness about its definition. People seem to identify more readily with happiness than with joy.

Happiness is created by the situation we find ourselves in at any given moment. I think it reflects external events and circumstances. We are happy if our children do well in academics or sports, happy for them and for us. We experience happiness when a situation provides the solution or result that pleases us and for which we were hoping. There is also a certain level of joy when, for instance, you have children, or later, when your child gets married and when they have children. There is also no question that there is joy in serving others.

Although helping others is pleasant, pleasurable, and provides a real sense of satisfaction, a lasting inward joy is completely different. I believe there is a much deeper kind of joy that has a spiritual component.

Out of interest, I asked friends to explain their understanding of happiness as opposed to joy. These are snippets from some of their answers: "Happiness is an emotional feeling in response to pleasant circumstances. Joy is a spiritual fruit that grows as you mature spiritually. It is not connected to circumstances." Another said, "I associate joy with a deep-seated contentment, a feeling of peace, faith, and trust. Happiness is a state of being at a certain time." And yet another explained it this way, "I can feel very sad and grieved over a loss in my life, yet still live in joy, because I know and can trust in God and can rest in his love and care in the middle of difficult circumstances."

Several friends indicated that joy goes much deeper than happiness and fills the whole person. Others felt that joy is a side benefit from knowing that God is in control, that he has shown us how things will end and has promised to be with us through all our circumstances, good or bad. Most friends indicated there was a spiritual side to joy.

I concur with their thinking. Joy is different from happiness. Joy emanates from deep within. It is created by knowing everything is settled in our minds and in our external situations. It comes from knowing everything is in order. Our hearts and minds are at rest because we have the assurance that all is well. It has the added ingredient of contentment; probably we should say spiritual contentment. I think this highlights the spiritual side to it. Maybe that is why it is so hard for people to define joy.

Dallas Willard, in his book *Life without Lack,* defines joy in this way. He says, "Joy is a pervasive sense of well-being that claims your entire body and soul, both the physical and the non-physical side of human self. Joy comes naturally when we are confident about who we are and what we are doing."[1]

Do you remember reading about the first Christmas, when Christ was born, the angels announced they were bringing a message of peace and joy which was for all people. Before Jesus returned to his father, he promised peace and joy to his followers. That peace and joy has been experienced by followers of Jesus ever since and is no less real today. When the spiritual side of us is satisfied and at peace, then a real deep joy resides there also.

Our Destination

The title of this chapter poses a question, an interesting question, "Where do we go from here?" Do you ever seriously think about that question? I refer, of course, to the end of this life. What happens when we close our eyes for the last time on this earth? Literally, "where do we go from here?" Obviously, this is not a subject readily discussed at the breakfast table. Most people would rather brush it under the carpet and hope that it goes away. Unfortunately, it doesn't go away, however much we ignore it. We are forced to face it at some point.

We all came into this world the same way and will exit the same way—all of us, no exceptions. One of the major unsettling aspects that prevents joy in life is not knowing when or how life will end, but it will happen eventually and inevitably for each of us. Then what? This is the part we would like to know is in order. I think we can know. Once that is settled in our minds then we will experience peace and joy.

Ignoring the certainty of our demise is universal. I guess it's fear of the unknown or just the fear of dying that causes most people to defer discussion of the subject. I am sure you have heard the saying, attributed to Woody Allen, "I am not afraid of dying. I just don't want to be around when it happens."[2] I am sure he echoes the secret desire of many people.

Death is no respecter of age. How often have we been shocked to hear that a young or middle-aged friend or work colleague has passed away from natural causes. Life is uncertain, our demise is not. I remember Winston Churchill being asked towards the end of his life, "Are you ready to meet your maker?" to which he humorously replied, "Yes, I am ready to meet my maker but is my maker ready to meet me?"[3] It was not long before he found the answer.

Some people like to think there is nothing at the end of life. We evaporate into nothingness. When we die, that is the end. We simply turn back into dust. Nothing but eternal blackness. But I believe evidence shows us differently, and that God created us to be more than just a physical body. We are spiritual beings as well. Why is it that millions of people constantly reach out to discover some spiritual connection outside of themselves? That alone would seem to indicate that within humanity there is an internal sense that there is something else, something more than this body or this life. There is, beyond doubt, more to us than what we see with our eyes. The Bible says that God *has set eternity in the hearts of men* (Ecclesiastes 3:11 NIV). This is probably why we have that inner sense of life after life.

I like what C. S. Lewis wrote in this connection. He said, "If we find ourselves with a desire that nothing in this world can satisfy, the most probable explanation is that we were made for another world."[4]

Although we cannot, and do not, base our belief system on the experiences of others, it's interesting that hundreds of thousands of people around the world have had a near-death experience, or as some people like to say, out-of-body experience. Although it is difficult to explain their experience or repudiate it, these people would certainly not agree that there is nothing at the end of life's journey. A common trait among them after their experience is that they no longer carry a fear of death. Those who indicated that they had visited "another place" say they experienced overwhelming love and the fact that they sensed they had arrived home. Most expressed they had no desire to return to their bodies.

Well-known doctors and surgeons, including Harvard specialists, who strongly believed that life ended at the point of death, had a complete change of mind after hearing firsthand accounts from their patients. Having conducted full-scale investigations into several thousand near death experiences, these medical professionals have been unequivocally convinced that there is consciousness after death.

Earlier in the book we talked about relationships. We mentioned that relationships within the family and with friends are essential and easily understood, but let's talk about a relationship with God. Is it really possible to have a personal relationship with the creator of the Universe? The answer is an unequivocal yes. A relationship with God and his son Jesus is the basis for the faith of Christians worldwide, who would testify to a life of joy. I believe we were created by God for God, and created

Invitation to Joy

to have a relationship with him, the ultimate purpose of which is to spend eternity with him.

It's All About Faith

I believe that one's faith is everything, which means faith is not just for when we go to a house of worship. Faith is not an add-on, an optional extra. It is an integral part of the whole, which means it doesn't just apply to some things and not to others in life or is just applicable sometimes and not at other times. To me, it's a twenty-four hour, seven-days-a-week faith. It's all or nothing. I do not believe in a faith of convenience. My faith is based upon a personal relationship with God and belief in the Bible. The Bible is God's Word to us. It has been verified as authentic historically, archaeologically, prophetically, but more importantly, its spiritual truth is being experienced by millions of people around the world today, just as millions more have in previous generations. People far more intelligent and better educated than me have given their lives for the truth of the Bible.

Right from the first few chapters of the Bible, we find it indicates God's desire to commune and have a relationship with humanity. He created us humans for that purpose. He walked and talked with Adam until he and his wife disobeyed God and were banished from the garden. It was they who created the enmity, the barrier, between God and humankind. Their disobedience brought about a chasm between God and humanity and severed the relationship God had originally intended. That severed relationship has passed on down to us. However, actions on God's side have always been there to eradicate the damage and to re-establish a relationship with us.

In the Bible, we find that all of us are invited to a personal relationship with God. It began with the Christmas story, the birth of Jesus, the Son of God coming to earth in the flesh. This was God reaching out to humanity. We read that Jesus was called Immanuel, which means, "God with us." Joseph and the shepherds were told that he would be called Jesus because he would save his people from their sins. The birth of Jesus and the death of Jesus were both within God's purpose to bring people into a personal relationship with him.

This was the very purpose of Christ's coming and dying. He came to remove that condemnation and eliminate the chasm between us and God. Jesus did that by taking our punishment for sin on himself and dying in our place. Thus, we can move from a state of separation from God to being totally forgiven and of becoming a child of God. One of the most well-known passages of the Bible sums up God's offer to us. It says, *For God so loved the world that he gave his one and only son, that whoever believes in him should not perish but have eternal life* (John 3:16 NIV).

Once we acknowledge our sin through a simple prayer of repentance, accepting God's invitation of salvation through Jesus, we move from the unforgiven state and come into the family of God. That's the new birth, when we begin our personal relationship with God. This is what God desires. He invites all people to come into his family. It is that simple. We cannot earn favour with God. God's love nullifies that. He loves us despite our wrongdoing. Doing good deeds is right and proper but it does nothing to create a relationship with God. The basis for our relationship with God has already been done through Jesus Christ, God's son, dying on the cross. We accept this by faith.

That's an abbreviated message of the Christian faith, which, when accepted, people become children of God, a wonderful parent-child relationship in which we can call him "Father." We become followers of Christ, God's son. As such, we are assured of God's care now and Christ's promise of spending eternity with him. With such a promise comes joy. We need have no more doubts about when or how our journey ends here because it turns into a transition as we move into God's presence. This is the promise made to all God's children. Thus, it brings peace and joy to know it is all settled.

Referring to his own death, Billy Graham said, "One day you will hear that Billy Graham has died. Don't you believe it. I shall be more alive than I am now. I will have just changed my address. I will have gone into the presence of God."[5] Dietrich Bonhoeffer said something similar when he was being led away for execution by the Nazis. He sent a message to Bishop Bell of Chichester which said, "This is the end—for me the beginning of life."[6]

Heaven

Heaven! It's that place that everyone seems to believe in, many expect to go there, but few people talk about it. Although the concept of eternity is hard for us to imagine, the Bible indicates that is what lies ahead of us, an eternity spent with God himself. It's true that we are given few precise details of heaven, but it certainly teaches that there is such a place for those who love God. Before he ascended from this earth, Jesus told his disciples, *In my Father's house are many rooms . . . I am going there to prepare a place for you . . . that you may also be where I am* (John 14: 2-3 NIV). With our earth-bound minds, we cannot even imagine what awaits those who are heaven-bound. We read, *No eye has seen, no ear has heard, no mind has conceived what God has prepared for those who love him* (1 Corinthians 2:9 NIV).

We learn from the Scriptures that it will be a place where there will be no more suffering, no more pain, no more tears, no more sickness or death, and no more grief. How it delights us personally to think that there will be no more Parkinson's, also no more cancer, heart disease, diabetes, or depression. There will be no more violence, abuse, murder, or mass shootings. There will be no more war. No more starvation or oppression. No more broken lives or broken homes. It will be a place of love, joy, and peace. It will be a place of such beauty beyond our imagination. It will offer a life that is more real than this one. We will work, worship, and serve. We will sense that it was a place made just for us, because we are made for heaven.

I believe, as followers of Jesus, we experience what the Bible indicates when it says, . . . *you believe in him and are filled with an inexpressible and glorious joy* . . . (1 Peter 1:8 NIV). For seven decades, I have been a Christian and I base the internal peace and joy in my life on that fact. Our life (meaning my wife Rita and I) has presented us with delights but also with obstacles and difficulties. Even now our life is not, as they say, "a bed of roses." However, the deep-down sense of joy has remained because we have been assured through our faith that God is in control and he will take care of every issue. We believe that, ultimately, he will put everything to rights.

I think there comes a time in life for many when they ask the question, "What is it I believe and why?" Most people will readily say they believe in God but often little beyond that. Some say, "I will consider this matter later in life." Unfortunately, we are not promised a "later" in life. One day I was talking to a gentleman about life after life, when he said to me, "I'll take my chances." In other words, I am good enough as I am. I don't need to make any special relationship with God. I am sure he is not alone in his thinking. Many people probably feel the same way. Obviously, we are all free to make our own choices, but we also need to be happy with the consequences of those choices.

If you have a prompting in your mind to consider the spiritual side of things in your life, then I would encourage you to follow that thought process and do something about it. It's between you and God. We alone can make decisions which affect our personal spiritual life. If you seriously and sincerely seek a relationship with God, then it will happen. I can assure you that God will direct you into that relationship. He will probably send someone across your path who will be able to answer your questions and give you guidance; it happens so often.

Life is a journey. I believe the pathway of life leads home. I look forward to seeing you there.

Afterword

So, there you have it, my observations on some aspects of life which I think give meaning and contribute to an enjoyable life. Considering the aspect of making other lives better, it's probably appropriate to ask ourselves the question, "If everyone did what I do, would the world be a better place?" What I have discovered is that our values dictate our actions. If we value kindness, we will look for opportunities to be kind. If we value generosity, we will find ways to be generous. So, I ask myself, am I looking for ways to be kind? Am I being generous with what I have? Do I have a caring heart? Am I showing a loving spirit? I am sure you have already practiced love and kindness and generosity in your life, all of which have brought you pleasure and a sense of satisfaction, in which case, this book was simply a reminder that the more we help others, the more we are helped.

I know I have emphasized the faith aspect and I make no apology for that because that is who I am. I think you have discovered that my faith is important to me. I recognize how it has been a stabilizing factor throughout life. Through the thick and thin of life, God has been there seeing us through. Not that we have always known it at the time, but looking back we see where he intervened for us. Our faith has been rewarded many times.

So, whatever you gleaned from this book, I hope it was positive and makes your days ahead even more pleasant and pleasurable. We get no practice run at life. This is it, so make the most of it, and may you truly experience the joy of living.

For your quiet contemplation, I will conclude with this very well-known prayer by St. Francis of Assisi.

Lord, make me an instrument of thy peace.
Where there is hatred, let me sow love,
Where there is injury, pardon,
Where there is doubt, faith,
Where there is despair, hope,
Where there is darkness, light.
And where there is sadness, joy.
O Divine Master, grant that I may not so much seek to be consoled, as to console,
To be understood, as to understand,
To be loved, as to love
For it is in giving that we receive
It is in pardoning that we are pardoned, and it is in dying that we are born to eternal life."[1]

Notes

Chapter 3.
1. Albert Schweitzer, *Speaker's Sourcebook 11* by Glen Van Ekeren, Prentice Hall, 1994.

Chapter 4.
1. Mother Teresa, Goodreads.com/Quotes/Inspirational.
2. Alan Paton, *Speaker's Sourcebook 11* by Glen Van Ekeren, Prentice Hall, 1994.
3. Roy Bennett, *The Light in the Heart,* Self-Published, 2021.

Chapter 5.
1. C.W.Vanderbergh. From one of his sermons in 2013.
2. St Augustine, Goodreads.com/Quotes/St Augustine.
3. William Barclay, *New Testament Words,* SCM Press, London, 1964
4. Mother Teresa, Goodreads.com/Quotes/Inspirational.
5. Rich Villodas, *Good and Beautiful and Kind,* Waterbrook, 2023.

Chapter 6.
1. Florello La Guardia story, *Speaker's Sourcebook 11* by Glen Van Ekeren, Prentice Hall, 1994.
2. Martin Luther King Jr., Goodreads.com/Quotes/Awareness.
3. J.R.R. Tolkein, taken from *The Hobbitt* but it is suggested it may be a quotation from the film as opposed to the book.
4. Albert Schweitzer, *Speaker's Sourcebook 11* by Glen Van Ekeren, Prentice Hall, 1994.
5. The young man in the church story was from Internet research.

6. The teenager on his bicycle story was from Internet research on Kindness.
7. The Bethany Moultry story was covered by the Press and on CNN.
8. Harold Kushner, AZ Quotes.com/Authors.

Chapter 7.
1. David Stendl-Rast, AZ Quotes.com/Authors.

Chapter 8.
1. The boy sacrificing his hair to help his mother's medical bills was from Internet research.
2. Brian Tracey, Goodreads.com/Quotes/Giving.
3. Mother Teresa, Goodreads.com/Quotes/Inspirational.
4. Winston Churchill, Goodreads.com/Quotes/Capitalism.
5. Robert G. Letourneau, *Mover of Men and Mountains*, Moody Publishers, 1967.
6. Oscar Saxelby-Lee story was covered by the BBC, June 2020.

Chapter 9.
1. Earl Nightingale, *Speaker's Sourcebook 11* by Glen Van Ekeren, Prentice Hall, 1994.
2. The hospital worker's story, *Speaker's Sourcebook 11* by Glen Van Ekeren, Prentice Hall, 1994.

Chapter 10.
1. The Amy Biehl story was written up in many places, one of which was the May 3rd, 2016, edition of the Orange County Register at www.ocregister.com.
2. Nelson Mandela, Goodreads.com/Quotes/Inspirational.

Chapter 11.
1. John Nichols, *The Nirvana Blues*, Ballantine Books, 1996.
2. Mario Raul de Morais Andrade, Information from Wikipedia.

Chapter 12.

1. Jordan Petersen, *12 Rules for Life - an antidote to chaos*, Random House, Canada, 2018.
2. Dr. Henry Viscardi, *Speaker's Sourcebook 11* by Glen Van Ekeren, Prentice Hall, 1994.
3. J. Sidlow Baxter, *Awake my Heart*, Kregel Publications, 1994.
4. Helen Keller, Goodreads.com/Quotes/Inspirational.
5. Gerry Lee's story was covered by *Time Magazine* in February 1981.
6. Helen Keller, Goodreads.com/Quotes/Inspirational.
7. Sue Richard's story, *Women's Devotional Bible*, NIV. p.1370.
8. Corrie Ten Boom, *Women's Devotional Bible*, NIV. P.1334
9. C. S. Lewis, Goodreads.com/Quotes/God.
10. Dietrich Bonhoeffer, Goodreads.com/Quotes/Inspirational.
11. Mother Teresa, *Speaker's Sourcebook 11* by Glen Van Ekeren, Prentice Hall, 1994.

Chapter 13.

1. Mark Twain, Goodreads.com/Quotes/Birth.
2. Winston Churchill, Goodreads.com/Quotes/Inspirational.
3. R. Buckmaster Fuller, *Speaker's Sourcebook 11* by Glen Van Ekeren, Prentice Hall, 1994.
4. The Ryan Hreljac story was written up in *The Globe and Mail*, 2010.

Chapter 14.

1. Dallas Willard, *Life without Lack*, Nelson Books, 2018.
2. Woody Allen, *Speaker's Sourcebook 11* by Glen Van Ekeren, Prentice Hall, 1994.
3. Winston Churchill, *Speaker's Sourcebook 11* by Glen Van Ekeren, Prentice Hall, 1994.
4. C. S. Lewis, Goodreads.com/Quotes/God.
5. Billy Graham, *A Gospel Coalition* Twitter entry in 2018.
6. Dietrich Bonhoeffer, Goodreads.com/Quotes/Death.

Afterword.

1. Prayer of St Francis of Assisi, Goodreads.com/Quotes/Aspirations/Prayer.

A word from the author...

If you have enjoyed reading this book and have found it meaningful, would you encourage others to read it also. You can do this by kindly going to Amazon.com, find the book and leave a sentence or two as a review? That would be very helpful, and I would appreciate it immensely. Let me thank you in advance for doing that.

John Murray

To connect with the author:
email: murray150@fastmail.fm
twitter: @AuthorJMurray
facebook.com/AuthorJohnMurray
website: http://www.jmurray.ca

To order more copies of this book, find books by other Canadian authors, or make inquiries about publishing your own book, contact PageMaster at:

PageMaster Publication Services Inc.
11340-120 Street, Edmonton, ABT5G 0W5
books@pagemaster.ca
780-425-9303

catalogue and e-commerce store
PageMasterPublishing.ca/Shop

About the Author

John has been married to his wife Rita for over 60 years. They have two children, five grandchildren and three great-grandchildren. Originally from the U.K. they now reside in White Rock, British Columbia, on the west coast of Canada.

Educated in England, John went on to study theology in Birmingham, U.K. and in Toronto, Canada. His life experience has been in business, in journalism, in pastoral ministry and overseas missions.

For the last twenty years before retiring he served as the Executive Director for Eurovangelism Canada, a mission working in Eastern Europe. He travelled extensively from Russia in the north to Albania in the south. Some of the stories in the book *Miracles: Coincidence or Divine Intervention* are from his days travelling in Eastern Europe.

His many years of speaking engagements took him to ten countries which included Canada, the United States, the United Kingdom, Europe and the Caribbean.

Since retiring in 2006 John has concentrated on his writing. *Invitation to Joy* is his sixth book.